More of HIM

RECEIVING THE POWER OF THE HOLY SPIRIT

More of HIM

RECEIVING THE POWER OF THE HOLY SPIRIT

GEORGE BLOOMER

WHITAKER
HOUSE

Unless otherwise indicated, all Scripture quotations are taken from the King James Version (KJV) of the Bible. Scripture quotations marked (NLT) are from the Holy Bible, *New Living Translation*, © 1996. Used by permission of Tyndale House Publishers, Inc., Wheaton, Illinois 60189. All rights reserved.

MORE OF HIM: RECEIVING THE POWER OF THE HOLY SPIRIT
Revised and Expanded version of *Empowered from Above*

ISBN: 978-1-60374-501-7
Printed in the United States of America
© 2002, 2006 by George G. Bloomer

Whitaker House
1030 Hunt Valley Circle
New Kensington, PA 15068
www.whitakerhouse.com

The Library of Congress has cataloged the hardcover edition as follows:

Bloomer, George G., 1963–
    More of Him : receiving the power of the Holy Spirit / George Bloomer. — Rev. and expanded ed.
        p.   cm.
    Rev. ed. of: Empowered from above.
    Summary: "Shows the importance of the Holy Spirit in a believer's life and discusses the baptism of the Holy Spirit, water baptism, and Pentecost"—Provided by publisher.
    ISBN-13: 978-0-88368-790-1 (trade hardcover : alk. paper)
    ISBN-10: 0-88368-790-9 (trade hardcover : alk. paper)
    1. Baptism in the Holy Spirit. 2. Christian life—Pentecostal authors. I. Bloomer, George G., 1963– Empowered from above. II. Title.
    BT123.B48 2006
    234'.13—dc22
                            2006017686

This book has been printed digitally and produced in a standard specification in order to ensure its continuing availability.

CONTENTS

INTRODUCTION

INTRODUCTION

Greater is he that is in you, than he that is in the world.
—1 John 4:4

Who is this *"greater"* One that John was talking about? It is the Spirit of Christ—the Holy Spirit! If you've surrendered your life to Christ, you have received the abundant gifts that His Spirit brings. The fruit of the Spirit—love, joy, peace, longsuffering, kindness, goodness, faithfulness, gentleness, self-control—is growing on the branches of your life. (See Galatians 5:22–23.) You live in an awareness of His presence and trust in the power that He gives.

Jesus Himself relied on the Holy Spirit as His source of power. Acts 10:38 says, *"God anointed Jesus of Nazareth with the Holy Ghost and with power: who went about doing good, and healing all that were oppressed of the devil; for God was with him."* What about you? Are you involved in the Father's business? Are you working for the kingdom of heaven with the same power that Jesus depended upon? Are you walking in His footsteps and carrying out the Great Commission that He left for His followers?

To be a witness for Christ, you must know who you are in Him. Those within the kingdom of darkness must also recognize who you are and where you stand. You need a reputation for having power and protection that comes from dying to self and living under the blood of your Savior. This assurance comes from the Holy Spirit. The repercussions of the power and protection that He gives are vast. As Acts 1:8 teaches, *"But ye shall receive power, after that the Holy Ghost is come upon you: and ye shall be witnesses unto me both in Jerusalem...and unto the uttermost part of the earth."*

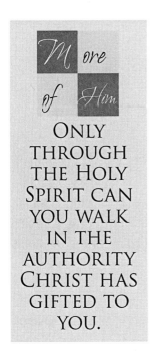

ONLY THROUGH THE HOLY SPIRIT CAN YOU WALK IN THE AUTHORITY CHRIST HAS GIFTED TO YOU.

It is only through the Holy Spirit that you can walk in the authority that Christ has gifted to you. Even in times of distress, when you don't quite know what to pray for because you're too distraught or too consumed with stressful situations, the Holy Spirit will step in and intercede for you. *"Likewise the Spirit also helpeth our infirmities: for we know not what we should pray for as we ought: but the Spirit itself maketh intercession for us with groanings which cannot be uttered"* (Romans 8:26).

Perhaps you've already begun to experience the fullness of the Holy Spirit. You've received baptism from above and have tasted the Spirit's filling in your life. You too must ask yourself, Am I doing the Father's business?

Simply receiving the Spirit does not ensure that you are walking in His ways. As Paul made clear in one of his epistles, having the Spirit's gifts in our lives means nothing if we don't show the Spirit's fruit as well. *"Though I speak with the tongues of men and of angels, and have not charity, I am become as sounding brass, or a tinkling cymbal"* (1 Corinthians 13:1).

Some years ago, not long after I had received the baptism of the Holy Spirit with the gift of speaking in tongues, I was selected by God to be carried in the spirit several times over the course of a month. During this time I received revelation on the heavens in the form of dreams. These dreams, which I later came to recognize as visions, came at the end of a fifty-day consecration fast leading up to the Day of Pentecost. With these dreams, it was as if the heavens opened up to me. God revealed much to me about the Holy Spirit, His nature, and His ways of working. This book records the contents of those dreams, as well as the understanding gleaned from them.

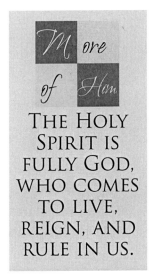

THE HOLY SPIRIT IS FULLY GOD, WHO COMES TO LIVE, REIGN, AND RULE IN US.

Through the revelation of this book, I pray that we will begin to understand the benefits of baptism in the Holy Spirit, in all its fullness. I pray too that we will not reduce it to an excuse for speaking in tongues, dancing around the church, or being slain in the spirit. Instead, may we recognize that the Holy Spirit is fully God, who comes to live, reign, and rule in us. He, the Spirit of Truth, is a teacher, a leader, an energizer of strength within our souls. May we rightly understand the Holy Spirit in the fullness of His character. May we yield ourselves to His working, as He moves in our lives according to His timing. The time has come to reject myths and to let go of questionable traditions. Allow scriptural knowledge to intervene, and learn what it really means to be baptized from above!

> *I pray for you today to be filled with all godliness and true revelation that can be released only through and by the Holy Spirit. I pray the convicting power of the Holy Spirit upon you that will destroy any stronghold that might be lying dormant in your life. Right now we claim this house—your temple—for the glory of God. We sweep it and cleanse it and forbid any demonic forces from returning to this place. Through the power and the anointing of the Holy Ghost, I pray for revelation knowledge to come upon you—the word of wisdom, the word of knowledge, and the word of prophecy—that healing will be your portion and deliverance your lifestyle. In Jesus' name, Amen.*

The Dream

SEVEN DAYS IN THE SPIRIT

The Dream

SEVEN DAYS IN THE SPIRIT

Day One

In my first dream I saw people standing all around the world. I could tell I was seeing the whole world because it was daytime in some areas and nighttime in others. The people wore many types of clothing as well. I recognized people from Turkey, Russia, Mexico, Palestine, Africa, and many other countries.

My dream was filled with music. I saw the heavens, or what appeared to be the heavens. I saw bouquets of color. Colors and colors and colors and colors were shooting out of the heavens. I can only explain what I experienced in terms of color and music. Some colors I can't even describe. I don't have words to tell you about the most beautiful yellows, greens, oranges, reds, and purples. Jasper. Ruby red. Emerald green. Magenta. Just colors, colors, colors. And the sounds were heavenly: trumpets, harps, drums, and violins.

When I passed through heaven's entrance, I saw more colors. The streets were pure, pure as can be. There was no crime. I heard voices, the many voices of my childhood as if kids were playing outside. As I walked through the streets, I drew nearer to what appeared to be ancient medieval buildings. They were all made of sapphire bricks. I have absolutely no idea what these monuments were. As I passed through the gate of the sapphire bricked walls, though, the voices changed. I heard voices of adults as they instructed their children, passing down their morals and values; voices of people talking business; and voices of thinkers discussing philosophies and ideas. Still, I could see no people.

I continued walking, guided by an inner-conscience, and approached what appeared to be a platform with steps, each step displaying colors of a heavenly rainbow. There were gifts too, wrapped up in the colors of Christmas, Easter, and Valentine's Day. Gifts were everywhere. Tons and tons and tons of them! The packages were of different sizes—some the size of cars, some the size of buildings, some as small as a calculator, and some the size of a shoe box—but all of them were wrapped up. And the voices changed; they said, "Where do we deliver this?" and, "Waiting on a pick-up." It was as if I were at a shipping company, looking at a graveyard of packages that had been misplaced and couldn't be delivered.

As I mounted the platform and left behind the unclaimed gifts, I passed through a door and suddenly began falling. It wasn't falling, though; I realized, instead, that I was being carried swiftly to another level by what appeared to be clouds. These clouds were not like the ones that hold rain and snow. Although they looked like clouds, they were made of a strawlike substance.

THE DREAM: SEVEN DAYS IN THE *Spirit*

As we descended to another level, I heard many noises—the sounds of eagles, wildebeests, seagulls, and bears, but no human sounds. Everywhere I looked, there was nothing but clouds set against the clearest white background. The noises grew louder as I descended. Finally, when I reached the ground, I saw creatures that must have been angels. It's extremely hard for me to describe the appearance of these incredible creatures. They weren't all in white apparel. The angels in my vision were dressed in several different colors, and I might add that color—yes, color—was the theme of this heavenly, angelic dream. I think I now understand why God went to such great lengths in Ezekiel 28 to explain Lucifer's covering, to give some clarity and information on what heaven was like and on the appearance of this creature.

The language of the angels seemed, to my human ears, to be a mixture of sounds made by different animals—like roaring, chirping, and hissing sounds combined with the noises from wildebeests, seagulls, and eagles. There were also sounds that I had never heard before.

There was a creature who looked like a man, with feet, hands, shoulders, and head. But when I looked closer at its head, it appeared to be composed of nothing but ears of different sizes. There was another creature with a man's body whose head was formed entirely of eyes—blue eyes, brown eyes, hazel eyes, green eyes—and the eyes were blinking. And I saw creatures flying from one side of heaven to the other; they all had several sets of wings, but appeared to have human bodies as well.

Though this may sound hideous, it was quite beautiful and fascinating. I don't know if this is how it is in heaven or whether God was simply showing me only what my human intellect could grasp. Then I saw the angel that had four faces—the faces of an ox, an eagle, a lion, and a man. When I beheld all this I remember saying, "I've read about this in the Bible." (See Revelation 4:7.)

And as two of those angels sped across the sky, I looked to see if they were holding a ring or a wheel like those described by Ezekiel. Although they moved across the open air in the heavenlies, they were not holding anything; they just moved about freely.

And then I woke up, fascinated by all that I had seen and heard.

Day Two

The dream I had the next night seemed pretty strange. It was as if the Spirit of the Lord was narrating and navigating me through a recapitulation of what I had dreamed the night before. I went through the rainbows, through the different sounds, the music, the steps of colors, the abundance of gifts, and the home of those creatures who made strange noises.

And then He put me back on earth again. When I "landed," I was sitting in a church with which I'm extremely familiar. There were people praying for the baptism of the Holy Spirit, tarrying for the Holy Spirit to come down. As I looked near the altar, there I was, on my knees, praying and tarrying for the Holy Spirit, pleading with God for something He so willingly and freely gives to everyone who simply asks of Him. I was begging and, in the dream, I heard the Lord say, "Beg not, but only ask, and I shall give it unto you. So shall it be yours." I remember stopping and asking God for it and feeling the presence of the Lord so strongly that I woke up. When I awakened, I wondered, "Am I hallucinating? Did I really just have a dream, or is this true?"

Later, when I went back to sleep, I returned to the altar in my dream where I saw myself begging, caught in somewhat of a tug-of-war. A young man in a suit approached me and said, "Let me show you the importance of receiving the baptism of the Holy Spirit." Suddenly I was standing in a completely white room without any furniture. The man stood before me and directed my attention to a balcony suspended over the entire earth. From the balcony I could see the principalities of Satan and a massive wall that Satan had erected around the entire earth. In every nook and cranny of the earth, he had demons, which were very frightening.

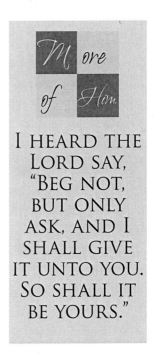

I HEARD THE LORD SAY, "BEG NOT, BUT ONLY ASK, AND I SHALL GIVE IT UNTO YOU. SO SHALL IT BE YOURS."

There were dark clouds and lightning hovering over the kingdom, as if there was an electric storm. And from under the satanic kingdom came a collection of beautiful lights in the form of blazing arrows, which traveled upward. "These are the prayers of the saints," an angel said.

I also saw disfigured creatures that were half-giraffe and half-elephant; half-woman and half-man; half-hyena and half-human. Everything was hideous and dysfunctional. It was as if an entire race had been annihilated and some Frankenstein had come to put it back together again, using bits and pieces from all over the earth. And the Spirit of the Lord told me, "These are demonic spirits who seek to embody men in the earth."

And that was it. I woke up. For an entire day I forgot the whole dream. Once I remembered, though, it frightened and quieted me. I was confused and excited, yet silent and still.

Day Three

Two days passed before my third dream came. In this dream, I looked up and saw saints everywhere, all around the world, praying at the same time. The prayers, which exited their mouths in the form of mist, traveled through ceilings, through the roofs of their cars, and up into the heavenlies. All the prayers appeared on television screens in the heavens where Satan had demonic forces watching the prayers as if they were observing Dow-Jones or NASDAQ results from Wall Street. The demons put checks next to each prayer, signaling whether or not they were going to let the prayers be released to heaven.

THE DREAM: SEVEN DAYS IN THE *Spirit*

And I saw a throne that was as white as snow and appeared to be pure. A man with white shoes, white socks, and white pants sat on this throne. I remember the pants were pressed so sharply that they looked like they could have cut someone. I did not see this man's face. I saw his head, though, and he had slicked-back, silken hair. His fingernails were well-manicured, and his right hand held three arrows.

The Spirit of the Lord said to me, "These arrows are the three musical spirits who have shaped modern culture." I beheld the arrows, and as I looked at them, physical heads appeared on each one: Boy George, Michael Jackson, and Prince, all entertainers who are unnaturally feminine in appearance and behavior. The arrows were given to a disfigured animal, a demonic spirit, who shot them at the earth in different directions. The arrows curved and turned, hit bull's-eyes, went through the bull's-eyes, and boomeranged back to the principalities, from where they were shot again. In the late 80s and early 90s, the music of Prince, Boy George, and Michael Jackson shaped the world. The arrows, upon hitting the bull's-eyes, released ungodly, off-key music, along with perversion, molestation, the stench of incest, and a number of other hideous spirits. The angel said, "As the culture changes, so shall the arrows change." And I propose to you today that there are demonic forces up in the heavens who now shoot the same arrows, only with the faces of different people of influence upon them.

After a while, I told my pastor about the series of dreams I was having and how I was not quite sure of what they meant. Thinking that perhaps the devil was disturbing my sleep, he prayed that I would not come under any further demonic attacks. However, when he related portions of my second dream in his sermon that next Sunday, our congregation erupted into a worshipful spirit that it had never quite experienced before. It was obvious that the message of my dream had the anointing of God upon it. The congregation burst into praise, and our morning service, which began at ten o'clock, didn't end until five o'clock that evening.

Excited with what God had done through the sharing of my dream, the pastor called me into his office to hear more. I can't explain what happened next except to say that at that very moment, the Lord took away the memory of my dreams. All I could tell the pastor was, "I'm sorry. I can't remember." For some reason the Lord wasn't ready for me to share any more at that time. Later, the memory of my dreams was restored, and the Lord led me to write them down. I can only pray that the movement of the Spirit that came upon the congregation that Sunday will be upon you as you read these words.

Days Four and Five

After my talk with the pastor, I went home and prayed that God would give me understanding and guidance on what I was going through. Shortly thereafter I had my fourth dream.

In this dream, the same man who approached me while I was at the altar praying in dream two came to me again. This time he announced that he was a messenger of the Lord and that he was going to show me great things. I went to a window, opened it up, and found myself on the same balcony from my earlier dream. Under the balcony were the words, "Balcony of Ages." And the man, who was an angel, said to me, "Before you are all the generations, and these are the spirits who will attack those generations." And then he showed me a great cloud, which came in a rumble, like someone playing a thunderous drum roll. The angel said there was a mighty force who would combat the forces of evil, and I knew what that power was— the Holy Spirit who would come in a mighty rushing wind.

The angel then took me briefly back to dream three to show me the demons standing around the walls. Then he led me to Calvary. I heard the nails ringing and the hammers pounding—bang, bang, bang. The crowd screamed and hollered, but I didn't see Jesus. I knew in my spirit, though, that I was at Calvary.

More of Him

THERE WAS A MIGHTY FORCE WHO WOULD COMBAT THE FORCES OF EVIL—AND THAT POWER WAS THE HOLY SPIRIT.

Soon there was a calm. Then the peace was shattered by screeching that came from a violin. I heard noises and voices again, as if I were back in the chamber from dream one. And the messenger of the Lord turned and said, "This is the age in which I will raise up my army."

I then had a tremendous revelation on the valley of dry bones, which Ezekiel had seen in a vision in Old Testament times. In this revelation, which came from my dream during night five, God showed me the valley of dry bones and then connected it to Pentecost, the captivity of Judah, and the declaration of Israel as a nation.

So I was on the Balcony of Ages. I saw the ages to come and all the demonic arrows and spirits that were directed toward it. But I heard a rumbling in the open air, and I saw this cloud of glory on its way. And the proclamation from the messenger of God was that this is the power that will combat the forces of the enemy. In my dream, this Scripture came to me:

And when the day of Pentecost was fully come, they were all with one accord in one place. And suddenly there came a sound from heaven as of a rushing mighty wind, and it filled all the house where they were sitting. And there appeared unto them cloven tongues like as of fire, and it sat upon each of them. And they were all filled with the Holy Ghost, and began to speak with other tongues, as the Spirit gave them utterance. (Acts 2:1–4)

It dawned on me that my dreams started on the commemorated Day of Pentecost, Pentecost Sunday. I realized that God was revealing to me the purpose of Pentecost—the purpose of 120 individuals in the upper room, the purpose of the outpouring of the Spirit. He was revealing to me how dirty vessels will be made clean and how, through His blood, He would take water and turn it into wine.

Scripture became so alive to me in my dreams that the rumbling of a great cloud beneath me became the moaning and groaning, the travailing of God in the Spirit, as He gave birth to the Holy Ghost on earth. He was waiting, though, for the 120 vessels to come together in one accord, in the same mind for a moment, so they could house His presence. He could then make His entrance onto the earth and combat the demonic forces of the ages that were eagerly waiting to attack the earth.

Through the propitiation and regeneration effected by the blood of the Lamb, the prophecy of a wedding at Cana had now come to pass on the Day of Pentecost. As recorded in the gospel of John, Jesus was invited to the wedding. When they ran out of wine, Jesus asked for six waterpots. These waterpots were nothing short of bathtubs where the people washed their feet after their long journeys on dusty roads. For the Scripture says, *"There were set there six waterpots of stone, after the manner of the purifying of the Jews, containing two or three firkins [twenty to thirty gallons] apiece"* (John 2:6). These pots were used for cleaning. And it was these—these dirty, dingy pots—that were brought to Jesus.

More of Him

DIRTY VESSELS WILL BE MADE CLEAN, AND THROUGH HIS BLOOD, HE WILL TURN WATER INTO WINE.

And He commanded them to be filled with water, representing life. Empty vessels were filled with water, life, the Spirit of God. The transforming power that took place at Pentecost was the same power Christ used when He turned water into wine. The Holy Spirit—pure, clean, and perfect—filled and transformed empty vessels, and He continues that work to this day.

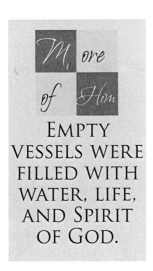

EMPTY VESSELS WERE FILLED WITH WATER, LIFE, AND SPIRIT OF GOD.

As the ruler or governor of the feast at the wedding tasted the wine, he remarked that they had saved the best for last, but the Scripture says he did not know from where the wine had come. He did not realize that this wonderful wine had, just moments before, been ordinary water. The Holy Spirit is coming in the most fantastic and awesome way to renew our vessels, our spirits, just as Christ renewed the water jugs on that day.

There is yet another wind to blow, another groaning. For the Bible declares in Revelation 7:1–4 that there are angels standing on the four corners of the earth, holding back the four winds of the earth, that it shall not blow on any tree or on the land until God has sealed the foreheads of His servants. The number that he heard was 144,000, and that 144,000 represents Israel in connection to the tribulation period that is about to come. I understood all this on the fifth night of my dream.

Day Six

About a week later, God took me back into the spirit realm. I was on the Balcony of Ages again, looking out over the earth as the saints prayed. On this night, though, my vision extended far beyond the Balcony of Ages. I was standing in the principalities and beholding the television screens, looking at the actual prayers of the saints as they reached the heavenlies. Moment by moment angels dropped down into the principalities, looking to the left and to the right and then falling down again to go into the earth. From time to time the angels would come out of heaven and into the principalities and look in both directions. But before they would make their next leap into the earthly realm, they would be snatched by demonic forces and held in a prison cell.

And the messenger of the Lord said to me, "This is the Word of the Lord coming live to you now. Have I not told you all this in the book of Daniel?" And my spirit quickened in the dream as I remembered Daniel 10:13, which tells about Daniel's prayer getting detained by the prince of Persia for twenty-one days. And God had to release an angel to fight, while a host of angels in the heavenly realm prayed, warring with the demonic forces to release the prayers of God's people.

Though this sixth dream was short, it was very revelatory. On this night I began to understand that God often answers prayers as soon as we send them, but oftentimes His answers and His blessings are blocked by another force in the heavenly realm. The saints need only to have patience and faith, and to know this principle:

If God's answer hasn't come, it will. Don't stop praising; don't stop praying; don't give up. Hold on because the angels of the Lord are wrestling for you.

Day Seven

My seventh dream came twenty days after the first night of dreams. I remember thinking, "Oh, Lord, I'm dreaming again." I knew something was happening, but I wasn't sure what. I didn't know if it was a dream or if it was a vision. I saw an enormous cloud being released. Then the messenger of the Lord said to me, "We must go to Calvary." And so we went back to Calvary. Once again I heard the unbearably loud screaming, the yelling, and the ringing of the hammer. Amid the noise and confusion, voices shouted out, "Give us Barabbas! Give us Barabbas!" I heard roosters crowing and voices crying, "I don't know Him! I don't know Him!" There were many voices.

More of Him

DON'T STOP PRAISING, DON'T STOP PRAYING, AND DON'T GIVE UP. IF GOD'S ANSWER HASN'T COME, IT WILL.

Then came the calm. The night changed to day as sunrise came. And there was violin music along with somber singing. I saw two women at the sepulchre; both were weeping and crying. And a messenger of the Lord said, "He is risen!"

This was love.

Then the scene changed and we were back on the Balcony of Ages. I looked down again and saw the cloud from before. It was now closer, and the sound from it was louder than before. There was wind with the cloud and something was going on around it really quickly. Lightning and flashing came out of it as it approached the balcony, and a whirlwind came out of it. Soon there was shaking and pieces of the building fell off.

Then, in the spirit realm, I saw everyone who was in the upper room. People were everywhere, filling the streets, and they were all speaking different languages. And everyone was reunited with his or her loved ones because there was an interpreter that wasn't there in times past. Peter stood up, saying, *"For these are not drunken, as ye suppose, seeing it is but the third hour of the day"* (Acts 2:15).

Then I looked up, and the messenger of the Lord said, "Behold, now: Satan's kingdom." And as I looked at Satan's kingdom and the principalities, there was mass confusion. Before, when the people prayed in their native languages, the demons had been able to write down what they said. On the Day of Pentecost, though, the saints stopped speaking their native tongues; they started speaking other tongues of men, and the door was opened for them to speak in the tongues of angels. And when they started praying in unknown tongues, the fallen angels could not unravel their prayers.

And God revealed to me that He had sent the Holy Spirit not only to comfort us, lead us, and guide us into all truth, but also to stop Satan from interfering with and hindering our prayer life. If ever there was a time for the body of Christ to rise up and understand the unseen power of the Holy Spirit, the hidden mystery of speaking in unknown tongues as the Spirit of God gives utterance, this is that time. The time is now.

Chapter One

THE PURPOSE OF PENTECOST

Chapter One

THE PURPOSE OF PENTECOST

*I*magine being one of the great great grandsons or ancestors of one the captives of Judah at the time when the book of Acts was written. They had heard the amazing stories of their forefathers as they so eloquently illustrated their experiences of living in a strange land after being carried away captive into Babylon. The grandfathers would have told of a great Messiah who was soon to come. He would bring with Him a Promise of Comfort. Hundreds of years have gone by. They had been hearing fabulous stories and prophecies, waiting in anticipation for what was yet to come. Then they heard of a remarkable party that was going on. It was reserved exclusively for 120 people who were strategically situated in an upper room. It was noised abroad that this party was going on, and the question that was buzzing in the air was, How are all of these Galileans having a party in our homeland—a place where we've longed for worship and waited for the coming of the Promise? *"Are not all these which speak Galilaeans?"*

What's more, the room was filled to capacity, and the multitudes were being turned away. *"There were dwelling at Jerusalem Jews, devout men carried out of every nation under heaven."* (See Acts 2:5–9.)

No doubt that in the midst were the descendants of the same men who had sat by the River Babylon, weeping when they remembered Zion, hanging their harps in the willow trees because their captives required songs of Zion. They were the ones who asked, "How can we sing the songs of Zion in a strange land?" (Psalm 137:2–4) No doubt some of these were the descendants of those who'd cried out, "The Lord turned again our captivity!" Now, though shocked and amazed, they rejoiced! Finally, they were coming out of captivity.

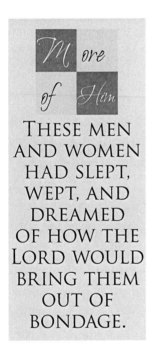

THESE MEN AND WOMEN HAD SLEPT, WEPT, AND DREAMED OF HOW THE LORD WOULD BRING THEM OUT OF BONDAGE.

These men and women had slept, wept, and dreamed of how the Lord would bring them out of bondage. Like many of us today, they couldn't imagine how the Lord would bring them out the bondage and the devastation that they had found themselves in, or for many of us, that we were actually born into. What a glorious day! What a glorious message to hear. What they thought was an out of control "block-party" actually turned out to be the Promise from on High—Beulah Land—that for years they had longed to see. Not knowing the language of that land, even a Mede, a Persian, or a dweller of Mesopotamia still heard the glorious gospel of Jesus Christ. And they accepted it because of the phenomenal way in which the Lord showed up on that faithful day—the sound of freedom, as a mighty rushing wind, filled the house. Cloven tongues, like fire, were everywhere, and in the midst of it all, the Spirit of the Lord announced His presence by filling those who were present in the room with His Spirit. *"And they were all filled with the Holy Ghost, and began to speak with other tongues, as the Spirit gave them utterance"* (Acts 2:4).

Many Christians sincerely hunger after a fuller, deeper experience of Christ; a hunger that stems from their desire to gain more knowledge of the Holy Spirit. It is on this path to receiving the indwelling of the Holy Spirit, however, that many believers become perplexed and confused about the baptism of the Holy Spirit. Though rarely dealt with, the indwelling of the Holy Spirit is an important topic, one closely related to the manifestation of the person of Jesus Christ; it deserves our full attention. The best place to start our learning journey is in Acts, where the Bible records the Holy Spirit's first indwelling of believers.

POWER IN THE UPPER ROOM

Thousands of years ago in an upper room, 120 men plus women came together at the command of the Lord Jesus. There they anxiously waited to be endued with power from on high. It was somewhat of a prayer meeting experience, where a number of individuals waited for God to appear to them again.

It's important to note that the manifestation of the Holy Spirit didn't come until Jesus had already returned to the heavens. In Acts 1:9 the disciples watched Him ascend on a cloud, the vehicle for His exodus to the heavens: *"And when he had spoken these things, while they beheld, he was taken up; and a cloud received him out of their sight."* Shortly after this, two visitors dressed in white apparel reminded the disciples that Christ would come again: *"Ye men of Galilee, why stand ye gazing up into heaven? this same Jesus, which is taken up from you into heaven, shall so come in like manner as ye have seen him go into heaven"* (Acts 1:11). The disciples knew to expect a return of the Lord's presence.

WE NEED TO BE EXPECTANT AND UNIFIED IN PURPOSE AS WE WAIT FOR GOD TO DO HIS WORK IN OUR LIVES.

In the upper room a number of things took place. First the congregation of the Lord assembled. They gathered together in unity of purpose. *"And when the day of Pentecost was fully come, they were all with one accord in one place"* (Acts 2:1). On the Day of Pentecost, the disciples, who believed Jesus' words and remained in Jerusalem to wait for His promise, were all together in one place. Even more significant, they were of one mind. This is a good reminder that some of us need to settle down, get in one place, set aside our differences, and let Pentecost fully come into our lives. Some people seek God so halfheartedly, without purposefulness, that they are completely unsure of His will for their lives. But God doesn't do a halfway job on anything. When God does something, He does it thoroughly and with expertise. We need to be expectant and unified in purpose as we wait for God to do His work in our lives.

Next in the upper room, the congregation prayed, as recorded in Acts 1:14: *"These all continued with one accord in prayer and supplication."* Don't miss the significance of what they did. In unity of spirit, they prayed and sought God. And finally they waited; they tarried for the Lord. They sat still until something spectacular and supernatural took place. It came upon them from above. In Acts 2, it happened; the baptism in the Spirit.

The baptism that took place in this room, however, was in no way comparable to the water baptism of John or even to our modern-day water baptisms in the name of the Father, the Son, and the Holy Spirit. This baptism was a baptism from above, a baptism of fire (see Matthew 3:11; Luke 3:16), not of water. It wasn't the emergence into water; it wasn't the sprinkling of water; it was the indwelling of the Holy Spirit—who came to live within the temple of the hearts of individuals.

And suddenly there came a sound from heaven as of a rushing mighty wind, and it filled all the house where they were sitting. And there appeared unto them cloven tongues like as of fire, and it sat upon each of them. And they were all filled with the Holy Ghost, and began to speak with other tongues, as the Spirit gave them utterance. (Acts 2:2–4)

As these seekers were earnestly asking and waiting, God provided two symbols of the Spirit's presence: the wind, which the Jews associated with the Holy Spirit— *"And suddenly there came a sound from heaven as of a rushing mighty wind, and it filled all the house where they were sitting"*—and fiery tongues, which divided and rested upon each one, showing that the Spirit's baptism included all—*"And there appeared unto them cloven tongues like as of fire, and it sat upon each of them."*

The Scripture then tells us that they were filled with the Holy Spirit and spoke in other tongues. *"And they were all filled with the Holy Ghost, and began to speak with other tongues, as the Spirit gave them utterance."* What does this mean? Does it mean the Christians at Pentecost began speaking like babies, practicing elementary babblings until they actually spoke something coherent? Or did they speak in other languages?

OTHER TONGUES

When the Bible declares here that these Christians spoke with other tongues, it means just that: They actually spoke other languages. Every man, regardless of his nationality, spoke in another language, witnessing to others and proclaiming the wonderful works of Christ. The "babble theory" is simply not scriptural, for the people who heard these Christians understood what they were saying. Why? Because each man heard his own tongue being spoken:

And they were all filled with the Holy Ghost, and began to speak with other tongues, as the

Spirit gave them utterance. And there were dwelling at Jerusalem Jews, devout men, out of every nation under heaven. Now when this was noised abroad, the multitude came together, and were confounded, because that every man heard them speak in his own language. (Acts 2:4–6)

THE SIGN OF TONGUES

Now let's look at the purpose that tongues served at Pentecost. The purpose for the sign—the gift of tongues—was to get the attention of the unbelievers gathered there so that they would listen. Paul acknowledged this purpose for tongues in 1 Corinthians 14:22: *"Wherefore tongues are for a sign, not to them that believe, but to them that believe not: but prophesying serveth not for them that believe not, but for them which believe."*

This certainly worked. All the different languages definitely caught the attention of those gathered there. They heard and saw things that they had never seen before, and they were astonished! How could these Galileans speak in so many different languages? Some even thought the apostles were drunk! Peter cleared up this misconception:

For these are not drunken, as ye suppose, seeing it is but the third hour of the day. But this is that which was spoken by the prophet Joel; And it shall come to pass in the last days, saith God, I will pour out of my Spirit upon all flesh: and your sons and your daughters shall prophesy, and your young men shall see visions, and your old men shall dream dreams: and on my servants and on my handmaidens I will pour out in those days of my Spirit; and they shall prophesy: and I will show wonders in heaven above, and signs in the earth beneath; blood, and fire, and vapour of smoke: the sun shall be turned into darkness, and the moon into blood, before that great and notable day of the Lord come: and it shall come to pass, that whosoever shall call on the name of the Lord shall be saved. (Acts 2:15–21)

Something awesome had happened. It wasn't a made-up show. In other tongues, these men of God spoke of His wonderful works. God showed up on the scene without anyone's help and filled them with the Holy Spirit, and they spoke in actual languages, in the known tongues of men.

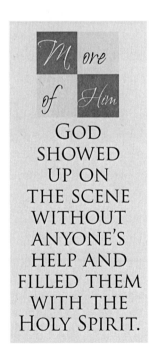

GOD SHOWED UP ON THE SCENE WITHOUT ANYONE'S HELP AND FILLED THEM WITH THE HOLY SPIRIT.

When the Holy Spirit speaks to a group of people, He will reveal God's will in various ways. If He so chooses, He will give the one He fills the divine ability to speak in a human language foreign to that person, just as He did on the Day of Pentecost. If He chooses, He will reveal a message through an unknown tongue in a spiritual language and accompany it with the gift of interpretation.

PROPHECY: THE "OTHER" SIGN

Peter reminded us in his powerful message that tongues are not the only sign of the Holy Spirit's presence; prophecy is as well: *"And it shall come to pass in the last days, saith God, I will pour out of my Spirit upon all flesh: and your sons and your daughters shall prophesy"* (Acts 2:17). So often we focus on tongues but ignore prophecy as a gift of the Holy Spirit. Scripture reminds us, though, that both are signs of the presence of the Holy Spirit. When Paul laid his hands on the converts, they spoke in tongues *and* prophesied. *"And when Paul had laid his hands upon them, the Holy Ghost came on them; and they spake with tongues, and prophesied"* (Acts 19:6). When Peter stood up to preach on the Day of Pentecost, he prophesied through a stirring sermon that won 3,000 converts to Christ (see Acts 2:41); Peter understood that Joel's prophecy was not completely fulfilled but only just beginning at that feast.

As that prophecy continues to be fulfilled today, we are going to experience an outpouring of the Spirit as never before. People who have never spoken English will speak English without learning it; others will speak in Russian, Greek, Hebrew, Chinese, Japanese—all kinds of tongues—without learning them. Unity in the body of Christ is also going to come. Thousands of people are going to be saved, and denominational differences will be set aside!

So whether the Holy Spirit works through actual human languages or through the heavenly language of angels, He won't speak to a group of people in a language

41

they can't understand unless it is to be interpreted. This is why He gave explicit instructions through His anointed minister concerning the use of tongues:

> *If any man speak in an unknown tongue, let it be by two, or at the most by three, and that by course; and let one interpret. But if there be no interpreter, let him keep silence in the church; and let him speak to himself, and to God.*
> (1 Corinthians 14:27–28)

Earlier in this same chapter Paul acknowledged the importance of ensuring God's order in the congregation through intelligent, understandable speech while also acknowledging the place of prophecy as well as private tongues for the purpose of revelation and edification:

> *For he that speaketh in an unknown tongue speaketh not unto men, but unto God: for no man understandeth him; howbeit in the spirit he speaketh mysteries. But he that prophesieth speaketh unto men to edification, and exhortation, and comfort. He that speaketh in an unknown tongue edifieth himself; but he that prophesieth edifieth the church. I would that ye all spake with tongues, but rather that ye prophesied: for greater is he that prophesieth than he that speaketh with tongues, except he interpret, that the church may receive edifying.* (1 Corinthians 14:2–5)

So Paul encouraged every Christian to be baptized in the Holy Spirit and speak in tongues, but only according to God's instructions. Notice what is happening in some churches today with regard to speaking in tongues, and consider whether it is done in the Spirit or the flesh. Many today are trying to be popular in religious circles instead of living and walking in the Spirit. Sister and Brother So-and-So might speak out in tongues they should have kept to themselves because they received no inspiration to move in the gift of speaking in tongues in the congregation with the interpretation mentioned in 1 Corinthians 12:

> *And God hath set some in the church, first apostles, secondarily prophets, thirdly teachers, after that miracles, then gifts of healings, helps, governments, diversities of tongues. Are all apostles? are all prophets? are all teachers? are all workers of miracles? Have all the gifts of healing? do all speak with tongues? do all interpret?* (vv. 28–30)

At worst, some speak in tongues merely to draw attention to themselves. There is no special revelation, no anointing, and sometimes these tongues even interfere with what the Holy Spirit actually wants to do.

On the Day of Pentecost, God chose to speak to the nations gathered there in each one's own language, as a sign to unbelievers of His presence on earth. His presence was confirmed through the symbolic signs of fire and wind, as well as through prophecy. From that day on the Spirit has continued to manifest Himself in various gifts of His own distribution. Through discernible speech and gifts, God's people can be intelligently instructed about His redemptive plans and purposes.

This is what really happened on the Day of Pentecost.

Chapter Two

WHO IS THIS HOLY SPIRIT?

Chapter Two

WHO IS THIS HOLY SPIRIT?

*But the Comforter, which is the Holy Ghost, whom the
Father will send in my name, he shall teach you all
things, and bring all things to your remembrance, whatsoever I have said unto you.*
—John 14:26

So, who is the Holy Spirit? Who is this Person who came on the Day of Pentecost? What is He like? Praise God He has not left us without answers to these questions! Praise Him that He has revealed to us the Holy Spirit through His most perfect and precious Word!

IN THE BEGINNING

*And the earth was without form, and void; and
darkness was upon the face of the deep. And the
Spirit of God moved upon the face of the waters....*

*And the L*ORD *God formed man of the dust of the ground, and breathed into his nostrils the breath of life; and man became a living soul.*

(Genesis 1:2; 2:7)

The Holy Spirit was with God from the start. As Genesis shows, the Holy Spirit was God's agent of creation, the breath of life from God into man. This beautifully mysterious nature of God is one of the most awesome and inexplicable revelations of the Bible: God in three persons—blessed Trinity! God the Father, God the Son, and God the Holy Spirit: They are one. This is hard for us to fathom. Three separate persons, united in one great Trinity. We must never try to separate the Three: The Father, the Son, and the Holy Spirit. They are one and have been so, all the way from time's beginning.

THE HOLY SPIRIT WAS GOD'S AGENT OF CREATION, THE BREATH OF LIFE FROM GOD INTO MAN.

*In the beginning God created the heaven and the earth. And the earth was without form, and void; and darkness was upon the face of the deep. And the Spirit of God moved upon the face of the waters....And God said, Let **us** make man in **our** image, after **our** likeness.*

(Genesis 1:1–2, 26, emphasis added)

Notice that God said, *"Let us,"* implying the presence of more than one Person in the Godhead. But how can this be? How can three persons be one? This is one of the many paradoxes, or mysteries, of Christianity. One way to understand it a little better is to think about water. Water is water, no matter what form it's in. It can be the liquid you shower in every day, the steam that comes out of your teapot, or the ice cubes you put in your orange juice every morning. Just as there are three separate forms of water, there are three separate persons in the Trinity. And just as all three forms of water are one hundred percent water, so too all persons of the Trinity are one hundred percent God. We may not completely understand it, but it's true. It's one of those things we just have to leave to faith.

Back to the beginning: In the beginning Adam was just a form—until God breathed life into him, until He breathed His Spirit into Adam's shell. Only then did he become a living soul. The Holy Spirit is God's life-giving wind, or breath.

As a descendant of Adam, you also are just a form until God breathes life into your nostrils. Physically alive, you might run, walk, talk, get dressed in the morning, go to work, hop on the bus to head for school—but you are just going through the motions until the Holy Spirit breathes His life into you. Until then, you are a mere form, bodily alive but not really living in the fullness of the Spirit.

How is this so? Because without the Spirit, you are spiritually dead. When Adam sinned, He died spiritually; consequently, all his descendants were born spiritually dead as well. Without the breath of God, or the Holy

Spirit, you are spiritually dead; you don't have the power to understand your origin, your purpose, or your spiritual identity.

CHRIST'S GIFT TO YOU

THE HOLY SPIRIT IS OUR COMFORTER, TEACHER, AND POWERFUL HELPER. OUTSIDE OF HIM, THERE IS NO LIFE.

God offers us everything we need to be spiritually alive. After Christ completed His work on the cross and returned to heaven, though, He sent *"another Comforter"* (John 14:16)—His Holy Spirit. Those who acknowledge Jesus as Savior can receive the Holy Spirit. And, beginning with this new birth re-creation, through the empowering of human beings with supernatural gifts, the Holy Spirit gives the power and ability to do the things God has ordained His children to do.

The Bible is clear; outside of Him, there is no life:

But ye are not in the flesh, but in the Spirit, if so be that the Spirit of God dwell in you. Now if any man have not the Spirit of Christ, he is none of his. (Romans 8:9)

Without the Spirit, we are dead spiritually. He is our Source, our spiritual Breath.

He is our Comforter, Teacher, and powerful Helper. He is here to assist us in our Christian walk with God.

He is here to help us even when we don't know how we—
or someone we are praying for—can best be helped:

> *Likewise the Spirit also helpeth our infirmities:*
> *for we know not what we should pray for as we*
> *ought: but the Spirit itself maketh intercession for*
> *us with groanings which cannot be uttered.*
>
> (Romans 8:26)

He is the Spirit of God who dwells inside those who
receive Jesus Christ as Savior and Lord, and He abides
with us forever because He is eternal. He is abiding in
you right now if you have asked Him into your heart. So
keep on reading to learn more of what all this actually
means.

HE SHALL TEACH YOU

Just as Jesus taught the disciples during His time
here on earth, the Holy Spirit also guides and teaches
those who belong to Him. Jesus said in John 14:26,

> *But the Comforter, which is the Holy Ghost, whom*
> *the Father will send in my name, he shall teach*
> *you all things, and bring all things to your remem-*
> *brance, whatsoever I have said unto you.*

The Holy Spirit works as a Guide, reminding us of
the things Jesus has taught, encouraging us to follow in
those ways.

The purpose of the Holy Spirit in your life is to teach
you God's truths and help you accomplish the things
God has called you to do. Oftentimes He convicts us of

sin or convinces us of certain actions we must take. So there really is no reason for someone who has the Holy Spirit not to know the truth.

Even people who have the Holy Spirit sometimes find themselves beginning to be drawn toward activities that are contrary to God's Word. If they are sensitive to the Spirit's voice, then they know that they are heading in the wrong direction. His presence within cautions them and they stop what they are doing; the Holy Spirit has convicted them that what they are doing is wrong. Praise God, though, that He uses our troubled consciences for His glory and our good. Such thorns drive us to Him for deliverance from sin and keep us humble enough to have patience with others who experience the same sort of struggles. Paul explained it best:

> *But I keep under my body, and bring it into subjection: lest that by any means, when I have preached to others, I myself should be a castaway.* (1 Corinthians 9:27)

Paul understood that without keeping himself subjected to the anointing of the Holy Spirit, where he could have a continued cleansing and deliverance, he'd be preaching deliverance to others while he remained bound.

ANOTHER COMFORTER

The Holy Spirit is not only a Convicter; He is a Comforter. Jesus described Him in this way in several passages recorded by John. We read:

But the Comforter, which is the Holy Ghost, whom the Father will send in my name, he shall teach you all things, and bring all things to your remembrance, whatsoever I have said unto you.

(John 14:26)

But when the Comforter is come, whom I will send unto you from the Father, even the Spirit of truth, which proceedeth from the Father, he shall testify of me: and ye also shall bear witness, because ye have been with me from the beginning.

(John 15:26–27)

Nevertheless I tell you the truth; It is expedient for you that I go away: for if I go not away, the Comforter will not come unto you; but if I depart, I will send him unto you.   (John 16:7)

Scripture also refers to the Holy Spirit as *another* Comforter, in fact, meaning He is a Comforter just as Jesus is a Comforter.

And I will pray the Father, and he shall give you another Comforter, that he may abide with you for ever; even the Spirit of truth; whom the world cannot receive, because it seeth him not, neither knoweth him: but ye know him; for he dwelleth with you, and shall be in you.   (John 14:16–17)

You probably have an idea of what the word *comforter* means. One definition of *comforter* is "a thick bed covering made of two layers of cloth containing a filling." We all know what this kind of comforter is. On a cold rainy day, or on a day when we're feeling tired and under the weather, nothing sounds as good as curling up in bed underneath a big, fluffy comforter. It warms us up and makes us feel better; it comforts us.

But even the softest blanket cannot compare to the comforting of the Holy Spirit. For when we talk about the Holy Spirit, the word *Comforter* means "helper; one who comforts." In this passage we just read, Jesus had told His disciples He was returning to the Father but that the Comforter, whom the Father would send in Jesus' name, would abide with them forever. Not only would He embrace them, console them, and make them feel better; He would help them, guide them, and lead them in truth and wisdom. Jesus said the Holy Spirit, the Spirit of Truth, would teach and bring to the disciples' remembrance all those things Christ taught during His time on earth. Jesus encouraged the disciples by assuring them that the Comforter would be with them. And that is why the Holy Spirit is sent to you: to come alongside you, to help you understand Jesus' teachings, and to enable you to do God's work.

You see, He's not just about giving you spiritual hugs when you're sad. He is your Teacher, your personal Trainer, your Encourager, your Discipler. Don't ever fall into the trap of believing He is *your* assistant to help you carry out *your* plans. Rather, the indwelling presence of the Holy Spirit is there to assist you in becoming more Christlike, to encourage you along the path of righteousness, and to equip you to be about your Father's business. (See Luke 2:49.)

Chapter Three

THE GREAT OUTPOURING

Chapter Three

THE GREAT OUTPOURING

ometime ago I was asked to preach at a conference in New Orleans, Louisiana. It was the month of July, six weeks prior to Hurricane Katrina touching down on the city and changing the lives of its residents forever. I remember entering the area that night where there were tens of thousands of people. I knew that whatever I'd be preaching that night would be very significant because as I proceeded to the platform to deliver the Word of the Lord, fear began to overcome me. I'd long been delivered from stage fright, but for some reason, on this particular night, it had come knocking on my door again.

As I prepared to deliver the Word, I began to feel many things on this very peculiar night. Although it was a clear and pleasant evening, I suddenly began to smell dampness in the air. As the old folks used to say, right before the storm would come, "I smell rain." Well, this is the same smell that I got a whiff of as I approached the podium to speak. Prior to entering the building that evening, I'd had a very wonderful and relaxing afternoon at the spa, swimming in the pool, and the pleasure of enjoying some scrumptious Louisiana cooking. It was strange to be suddenly confronted with anything but ease when the time came to do what I enjoyed doing the most—which is ministering to God's people. I was a bit perplexed, to say the least, by what I was feeling and experiencing at that time. In addition to smelling rain and feeling dampness in the air, I also began to hear howling, though not the howling of an animal, but more like that of a mighty rushing wind, as spoken of in Acts chapter two.

> THE BAPTISM OF THE HOLY SPIRIT IS THE POWER OF THE HOLY SPIRIT WHO LEADS AND GUIDES US INTO ALL TRUTH.

Suddenly it hit me—this must be the message for the night! The power of the gift of the Holy Spirit has many benefits and without it we are limited in our spiritual insight. What we hear and see through the eyes of the Holy Spirit is much more real than what reality allows us to witness with our physical eyes.

The baptism of the Holy Spirit is not just for us to speak in tongues or to prophecy, but it is the power of the Holy Spirit who leads and guides us into all truth. He gives us wisdom, which exceeds human knowledge, anoints us to raise our children, to be good husbands or wives. Nothing is too great or small for the Holy Spirit when we earnestly seek Him in truth. Furthermore, He allows us to become partakers of His power as a gift that He has left as an inheritance for His children.

God uses the Holy Spirit to anoint us for every task. Mary was anointed to conceive and bear the sacred birth of Jesus Christ. Jesus was anointed by the Holy Spirit to endure the suffering of the cross. And I'd been anointed on that faithful night in July 2005 by the Holy Spirit in an arena to minister to the needs of thousands of people, six weeks prior to Hurricane Katrina hitting the city of New Orleans. After ministering that night, thousands received the baptism of the Holy Spirit. They gave witness and testified of the power of His presence as He took up residence within them to fill the voids that had been missing within their individual lives.

At the time, I did not know that the rain I smelled would soon be a physical torrential rain. Nor did I realize that the howling I'd heard in the spirit would be the howling of the wind trapped between buildings that it would ultimately tumble to the ground. One thing I did know, however, was that the Lord was equipping the body of Christ to endure some attacks that were about to come.

John first introduced this power in Matthew 3:11.

I indeed baptize you with water unto repentance: but he that cometh after me is mightier than I, whose shoes I am not worthy to bear: he shall baptize you with the Holy Ghost, and with fire.

59

More OF HIM

WATER BAPTISM

In the verses that precede verse 11 in Matthew chapter three, John the Baptist is seen admonishing the people to repent. Notice in verse six that as they were being baptized in water, the people were first repenting of their sins.

When John noticed the Pharisees and Sadducees observing, he immediately began to rebuke them and warn them to repent. He testified to them of God's power above that of Abraham, himself, and anyone they have ever known. He spoke to them about the authority of Jesus to cast down everything that is not like Him. John the Baptist then reiterated the fact that although he baptized with water, another was coming after him endowed with power to baptize them with fire.

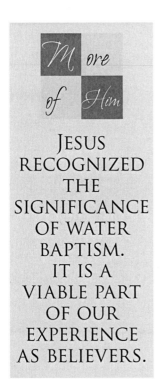

JESUS RECOGNIZED THE SIGNIFICANCE OF WATER BAPTISM. IT IS A VIABLE PART OF OUR EXPERIENCE AS BELIEVERS.

This fire that John was referring to was the power of God—the Holy Spirit. Jesus Christ came to be baptized in water by John the Baptist. Surely if Jesus Himself recognized the significance of water baptism, we too should recognize it as a viable part of our spiritual experience as believers in Christ Jesus.

TWO WOMEN, TWO BOYS

The Bible story of the relationship between Jesus and John begins when they were both still in the womb. Zacharias, John's father, was approached by the angel Gabriel and told that his wife, Elizabeth, although she was barren, was going to bear him a son. Six months later, Gabriel appeared again, but this time to Mary. He announced to Mary that she had found favor with God and, although she was a virgin, she was going to bring forth a Son and name Him Jesus. (See Luke 1). Gabriel then informed Mary of the miracle that her cousin Elisabeth was about the bear a son as well: *"Behold, thy cousin Elisabeth, she hath also conceived a son in her old age: and this is the sixth month with her, who was called barren"* (Luke 1:36). Upon hearing the news, Mary hurried to her cousin Elisabeth's house.

> *And it came to pass, that, when Elisabeth heard the salutation of Mary, the babe leaped in her womb; and Elisabeth was filled with the Holy Ghost.* (Luke 1:41)

Not only did the two mothers come in contact with each other, but the presence of John and Jesus collided as well. At the presence of Jesus, John leapt in his mother's womb. Thirty years go by and the two met up again at the River Jordan.

Both of these women bore children miraculously, and both experiences have many other striking comparisons:

1. Both women had boys.

2. Both were foretold of their conceptions by the angel Gabriel.

3. Both were told the names of the children before they were born, Elizabeth's son would be John, and Mary's Son would be called Jesus.

4. Both were told of the greatness that would accompany each child: Mary carried the Son of the Most High; and Elisabeth carried John, who would prepare the way for Jesus.

After Jesus was baptized by John at the River Jordan, the heavens immediately opened. The Spirit of the Lord descended like a dove, and an announcement was made by God for all to hear and see: *"This is my beloved Son, in whom I am well pleased"* (Matthew 3:17). Jesus received power to confront satanic forces.

THE POWER OF PRAYER

Following this powerful experience, Jesus was then led by the Spirit into the wilderness to be tempted by the devil. When Jesus went into the wilderness He fasted and prayed for forty days and forty nights. Notice that His initial purpose for going into the wilderness was not to fast and to pray, but He was led into the wilderness to be tempted of the devil. The trying of His faith was to prepare Him for the patience that He was going to need in order to endure the suffering of the cross. But Jesus ended up praying and fasting for forty days and forty nights.

Scripture teaches that we ought to always pray and not faint. Constant prayer does not suggest that we spend twenty-four hours a day in ritualistic prayer, but rather that we have a conscious awareness of God dwelling with us and in us all day and at all times. This conscious awareness gives us an audience with God and access to God's library of revelation. At all times, those of us who are filled with the Spirit of God may slip into a supernatural place and draw from His revelatory wisdom, which will ultimately bless those around us as well. This is why people who pray and fast have supernatural wisdom and insight that those who don't spend time with God do not possess.

More of Him

CONSTANT PRAYER SUGGESTS THAT WE HAVE A CONSCIOUS AWARENESS OF GOD AT ALL TIMES.

Jesus was led by the Spirit into the wilderness to be tempted by the devil. But instead of waiting for the tempter to come to Him, Jesus did what He knew would work for Him, and that was to pray. So He prayed to God. Satan waited forty days and forty nights to begin his temptation. *"He that dwelleth in the secret place of the most High shall abide under the shadow of the Almighty"* (Psalm 91:1). As Jesus abided in the secret places with the Father through fasting and prayer, He was covered by the shadow of His mighty hand.

There is a secret place, a secret chamber, and it is revealed to us when we pray, when we fast, and when we worship. Notice that when the Holy Spirit was leading Jesus to be tempted and tried by the devil, Jesus prayed: *"The effectual fervent prayer of a righteous man availeth much"* (James 5:16). Scripture does not actually tell us what Jesus prayed, but may I suggest to you that the prayer may have gone something like this: "Father, I want to know more of You. Lord, as I spend this time with You, I ask that You lead Me and guide Me into all truth. Keep Your hands on Me as Your will is perfected through Me, Your Son Jesus." After He prayed and fasted forty days and forty nights, Jesus then hungered. Now, Satan, who had been waiting all that time for the perfect opportunity to tempt Jesus, saw what he felt was a crack in the door to get to Jesus.

SATAN'S TACTICS

Therefore Satan said, "I will use His appetite against Him." So the first thing that Satan said to Jesus was, *"Command that these stones be made bread"* (Matthew 4:3). Bread symbolizes all that sustains life. Satan wanted our Lord and Savior to submit to his trickery during Jesus' vulnerable state of hunger. When the Lord God cursed the serpent in Genesis 3:14, He said, *"On your belly you shall go, and you shall eat dust all the days of your life"* (NKJV).

The word *"belly"* is symbolic of one's appetite. So when Jesus had completed His time of praying and fasting, and Satan approached Him, saying, "Command these stones to be made bread," the devil was, in a sense, attempting to curse Jesus by the same curse that had been inflicted upon him in the garden of Eden. He wanted to take Jesus from His exalted place in God to a belittled state by making Him bow to His belly, His appetite. First Corinthians 10:7 warns us of the lust of filling the belly above the desire of pleasing God: *"Neither be ye idolaters, as were some of them; as it is written, The people sat down to eat and drink, and rose up to play."* But Jesus turned to Satan and said, *"It is written, Man shall not live by bread alone, but by every word that proceedeth out of the mouth of God"* (Matthew 4:4). Man shall not live by his daily sufficiency, but he shall live by the word that God has previously spoken concerning him: Where God guides, He provides.

Then, Satan took Jesus out on a high pinnacle at the top of the temple and said, *"If thou be the Son of God, cast thyself down: for it is written, He shall give his angels charge concerning thee: and in their hands they shall bear thee up, lest at any time thou dash thy foot against a stone"* (Matthew 4:6). Jesus responded, *"Thou shall not tempt the Lord thy God"* (verse 7).

Finally, as a last attempt, the devil tried to get Jesus to enter into idol worship. He took Him to a high mountain to see all the kingdoms of the world and said, *"All these things will I give thee, if thou wilt fall down and worship me"* (verse 9). So there were three things that Satan used in an attempt to destroy the ministry of Jesus, and these are the same things that he uses against us today:

1. Turn the stones to bread—The devil causes us to become so focused on fulfilling the needs of our appetites that we become so distracted we're unable to hear the voice of God.

2. Cast Himself from a high pinnacle—The devil loves it when we cause ourselves self-inflicted pain or we tempt God.

3. If you worship me, I will give you the kingdoms of the earth—The devil plays to our egos in an attempt to get us to fall into idol worship. Anything that he can find to divert our attention away from God, he will use for our demise.

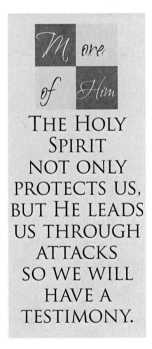

THE HOLY SPIRIT NOT ONLY PROTECTS US, BUT HE LEADS US THROUGH ATTACKS SO WE WILL HAVE A TESTIMONY.

Jesus recognized that He was dealing with Satan and rebuked him. The devil finally left, and the angels of the Lord came to minister to Jesus. Notice that the indwelling of the Holy Spirit not only protects us against the attacks of the enemy, but He sometimes leads us and guides us to defeat the satanic strategies so that we will have a testimony to deliver to our brothers and sisters during their future attacks. *"They overcame him by the blood of the Lamb, and by the word of their testimony"* (Revelation 12:11).

The baptism of the Holy Spirit provides us with power because...

1. Baptism gives you a heavenly proclamation of an earthly stand.

2. Baptism in the Holy Spirit gives you a Tour

Guide who leads you and guides you into all truth.

3. The Comforter comforts you during very difficult and frightful times in the present and also warns you of difficult times to come.

4. He will equip you with a language that will edify, or build you up.

5. He will anoint you for every task. So where there is only one initial filling, there are many refreshings in the Holy Spirit to refresh you.

So when God spoke to Jesus and said, "You are My beloved Son in whom I am well pleased," it was the anointing of the Lord going forth, preceding the forty days and the forty nights—during the season that He would be tempted by the enemy. But when the season had passed, the angels of the Lord came to refresh Jesus and fill Him with the presence of the Lord for His next assignment.

Baptism in water and baptism in the Holy Spirit are both powerful and vital components in the believer's life. For the purpose of dispelling the myths that accompany thethe baptism of the Holy Spirit, let's take a more in-depth look at it.

BAPTISM IN THE HOLY SPIRIT

When John the Baptist spoke of the power to come, he was preparing the people for things to look forward to. While he wanted to express the importance of this significant moment, as he baptized believers with water, he also wanted to make sure that they understood that One much more significant than him was to come. John the Baptist wanted the people to realize his limitations while understanding the infinite power of the Holy Spirit.

In Acts 1:5 Jesus testified of His own power: *"For John truly baptized with water; but ye shall be baptized with the Holy Ghost not many days hence."* Remaining true to His word, Acts chapter two shows the Word of the Lord coming to pass. When others witness you operating in the power of the Holy Spirit it encourages them to believe.

> *More of Him*
>
> THOSE WHO ARE TRULY FILLED WITH THE SPIRIT OF GOD HAVE A PRESENCE THAT LEAVES A LASTING IMPRESSION.

Those who have the gift of the Holy Spirit are blessed with supernatural insight that's not always readily available to those who are not baptized in the Holy Spirit. Whenever you encounter those who are truly filled with the Spirit of God, you notice that the presence of these individuals leaves a lasting impression that remains long after they've physically left your presence. The person isn't what draws your attention. Instead, it is the spirit of God that resonates from the inside out, draws you to those who walk in the Spirit, and leaves an indelible impression for days to come. It is not something that can be faked or forged.

So powerful is the gift of the Holy Spirit that John the Baptist likened the power of the Spirit to fire. The

Holy Spirit is like a consuming fire that burns until it purges out of you what's not like God and leaves you with an everlasting mark of having been touched and altered by His very presence from on High. That is the internal and life changing experience that the Holy Spirit leaves behind. Externally, however, He also leaves signs of His presence. You may not be able to physically see Him, but you may feel His presence and you can be sure that He is always around.

Much like the wind that blows through the leaves on a brisk afternoon in Fall, you can't see it, but you know that the wind is there by the altering of the leaves, which have no choice but to respond to its command. As the wind blows, the leaves are seen turned inside out as they acquiesce to the wind's demands. And so it is with the Holy Spirit. He holds the capacity to turn you inside out so that whatever's lurking within you that is not like Him will be shaken. Perhaps God is shaking up some things in your life at the present time. Rest assured that it is not for your demise but for the perfecting of your character and that His glory may be magnified to those who might not yet believe.

> *The wind bloweth where it listeth, and thou hearest the sound thereof, but canst not tell whence it cometh, and whither it goeth: so is every one that is born of the Spirit.* (John 3:8)

Outwardly, onlookers can hear and see the effects of the Holy Spirit. When others see those who are born of the Spirit magnifying God and prophesying according to His power, they immediately recognize that the joy they're witnessing is not birthed from earthly and material gain. They begin to desire that same joy and want the same peace that allows a Spirit-filled Christian to rejoice even in the midst of pain. You never know who is watching you and drawing strength from the Christ that's resonating from you, all because of your belief.

Jesus said that one of the signs to follow those who believe is, *"In my name shall they cast out devils"* (Mark 16:17). In the Old Testament, they did not cast out devils, but in the New Testament, devils are subject to His name. I remember preaching to a congregation years ago regarding the authority that we have in the name of Jesus. As I preached, I kept noticing a young lady in the balcony who would stand up, sit down, stand up, and sit down again. Because of the awkwardness of her movements, every time she did this, it got my attention. Nonetheless, I continued preaching, and there was an amazing outpouring of the Holy Spirit. Demons were cast out, people began speaking in tongues, being filled with the Holy Spirit, and calling on the name of Jesus.

After the service, a young lady asked if she could borrow a few minutes of my time to speak to me regarding what had happened to her during the service. As she entered the pastor's study, I noticed that she was the same young lady whom I'd seen in the balcony while I was ministering, getting up, and sitting down over and over again at the beginning of the service. She entered the office and began explaining to me what was going on within her during this time. She stated that as the Word of God was going forth, a voice began to speak to her. This demonic voice began telling her to get up and cast herself down from the balcony in order to stop the service from going forth. She also stated, however, that every time she got up to jump, it felt like an unknown force was yanking her back down into her seat. As the service continued, she was delivered and set free by the power of God.

The devil knew that a great outpouring was about to take place and he attempted to hinder this service by taking the life of an individual to do so. The devil will go to any extreme to keep the gospel from being preached. This is why you can never allow him to distract you from delivering the Word of the Lord and from seeing the purpose and call of God upon your life from being fulfilled.

It's often not what you say that makes the difference, but your actions and reactions to life that ultimately draw the picture for others of who Christ is and His omnipotence. Because you are born of the Spirit, the unbeliever may not quite understand what exactly is drawing him or her to you, but these individuals do recognize that what they see, hear, and feel from your spirit is something that they lack, yet very much desire to have.

> *While Peter yet spake these words, the Holy Ghost fell on all them which heard the word. And they of the circumcision which believed were astonished, as many as came with Peter, because that on the Gentiles also was poured out the gift of the Holy Ghost. For they heard them speak with tongues, and magnify God.* (Acts 10:44–46)

The power of the Holy Spirit is so consuming that He leaves a lasting effect upon all who come in contact with Him. In Acts chapter ten we see that when the gift of the Holy Spirit fell, His Spirit was even poured out onto the Gentiles and they began to manifest His Spirit by speaking in tongues and magnifying God. The Jews were astonished when they heard the Gentiles speak with tongues.

Many controversial statements have been made concerning the indwelling of the Holy Spirit that often keep people from experiencing the full manifestation of the power of God. For instance, after you receive the Lord as your personal Savior through faith and confession, it is true that you have received the Holy Spirit in one capacity, but you could possibly still lack the full manifestation of His power in another. Why? Because you have not yet been baptized in the Holy Spirit. To be baptized in the Holy Spirit is what John the Baptist was referring to in Matthew 3:11: *"he that cometh after me is mightier than I, whose shoes I am not worthy to bear: he shall baptize you with the Holy Ghost, and with fire."*

THE FIRE OF HOLY SPIRIT CONSUMES ANYTHING THAT PROVES VULNERABLE TO ITS FLAMES.

The fire of the Holy Spirit consumes anything that proves vulnerable to its flames. When Jesus baptizes you with the baptism of the Holy Spirit, He is swift and powerful, consuming everything that's not like Him, while preserving the best of you in the process. This is why those who are baptized in the Holy Spirit are so keen to the devices of Satan. It's because they're not operating out of their own knowledge, but they're under the authority and spiritual unctioning of God.

On resurrection Sunday, the disciples had an encounter that would not only change their lives, but one that would prove as a lasting effect on generations to come. In John 20:21, Jesus appeared before the disciples for the first time after He'd been resurrected. *"Then said Jesus to them again, Peace be unto you: as my Father hath sent me, even so send I you."* The presence of God ushers in the peace of God to all who come in contact with Him. Furthermore, after He blesses you, He sends you—those who have been endowed by the Holy Spirit's power—to be a blessing to others.

"And when he had said this, he breathed on them, and saith unto them, Receive ye the Holy Ghost." The Spirit of God is the breath of life. Here we see history in the making as the disciples receive the gift of the indwelling of the Holy Spirit. In the Old Testament there were prophecies that foretold of

More of Him

AFTER GOD BLESSES YOU, HE SENDS YOU TO BE A BLESSING TO OTHERS.

this experience, but now in the New Testament we see the disciples actually living out the prophetic Word of God, not only as it relates to receiving the Holy Spirit baptism, but also as it relates to their salvation.

As previously stated, salvation requires two components: faith and confession. If you believe, according to

Romans 10:9, that God has raised the Lord Jesus from the dead and confess this fact with your mouth, salvation is yours. After the disciples' encounter with Jesus subsequent to His resurrection, they now believed that He'd been raised from the dead. This had been the missing component to complete their salvation. They were now born again and blessed with eternal life. *"The Spirit is life because of righteousness"* (Romans 8:10).

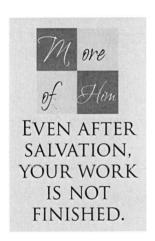

EVEN AFTER SALVATION, YOUR WORK IS NOT FINISHED.

Righteousness is attributed to those who believe that Christ died on the cross and rose again. At their rebirth, Jesus breathed upon them the breath of life as they received the indwelling of the Holy Spirit. In Luke 24:49, Jesus ordered the disciples to *"tarry in the city of Jerusalem until you are endued with power from on high"* (NKJV). Weeks later, *"they were all filled with the Holy Spirit and began to speak with other tongues, as the Spirit gave them utterance"* (Acts 2:4 NKJV).

To differentiate Resurrection Sunday from Pentecost Sunday, observe the following chart:

Resurrection Sunday (John 20)	Pentecost Sunday (Acts 1–2)
Christ is raised from the dead.	Christ ascends into heaven.
He breathes on the disciples and tells them to "receive the Holy Ghost." The disciples believe.	*...they were all filled with the Holy Ghost...* (This is the indwelling of the Holy Ghost, which can only be experienced after salvation).
The outcome is the gift of eternal life.	As a result they were endowed with Power—the power that Jesus had foretold them of in Luke 24:49.

The question is often asked, "Can a person be saved without being baptized in the Holy Spirit?" The answer is, "Yes." In Acts 8:14 we see that the Samarians had already *"received the word of God."* They believed in the resurrected Christ and had even been baptized. They were saved but had not yet been baptized with the Holy Spirit. Therefore, the apostles sent to them Peter and John,

> *Who, when they were come down, prayed for them, that they might receive the Holy Ghost: (For as yet he was fallen upon none of them: only they were baptized in the name of the Lord Jesus.) Then laid they their hands on them, and they received the Holy Ghost.* (verses 15–17)

There are three pertinent experiences that have a lasting effect on your life as a believer. You hear the Word of God being preached and it begins to prick your heart.

1. As a result, you believe.

2. You are saved.

3. You receive the indwelling of the Holy Spirit.

Time and time again, Scripture shows that the indwelling of the Holy Spirit cannot happen without salvation preceding. Simon the sorcerer found this out when he attempted to use money as a means of acquiring the gift. *"And when Simon saw that through laying on of the apostles' hands the Holy Ghost was given, he offered them money, saying, Give me also this power, that on whomsoever I lay hands, he may receive the Holy Ghost"* (Acts 8:18–19). Peter rebuked Simon and admonished him to repent. The gifts of God cannot be purchased or acquired through earthly means. Simply call upon the name of Jesus earnestly and receive His great outpouring in the Spirit.

Chapter Four

WHY TONGUES?

Chapter Four

WHY TONGUES?

I remember growing up in the church as a young
boy, struggling with my understanding of the
gift of tongues. Having been raised in a Seventh-day Adventist church, I found it especially difficult
to comprehend this unusual means of communicating
with God. I had no understanding of the charismatic
experience, and the idea of speaking in tongues only left
me dumbfounded. How could anything of this nature
usher anyone into the heavens, into spiritual and intimate conversation with God Almighty Himself?

After I was saved and converted to Pentecostalism,
however, I found out that salvation was not enough. I
longed for a deeper power to fill the void within whenever my initial zeal had ceased. Jesus said, *"Ask, and it
shall be given you; seek, and ye shall find; knock, and
it shall be opened unto you"* (Matthew 7:7). So I did just
that; I was baptized with water, then received the baptism of the Holy Spirit, and immediately the experience
of tongues came to me.

Speaking in tongues, however, is not to be confused with the initial evidence of being filled with the Holy Spirit. To imply that a person is not filled with the Holy Spirit because he or she does not speak in tongues is unsound teaching. Nowhere does the Bible say that speaking in tongues is the initial evidence of the Holy Spirit; instead, it continually talks about being endued with power from on high.

POWER FROM ON HIGH

The only clear spiritual evidence of baptism in the Holy Spirit is the endowment of power:

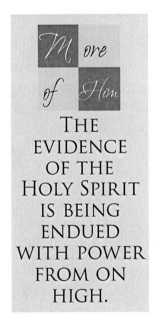

THE EVIDENCE OF THE HOLY SPIRIT IS BEING ENDUED WITH POWER FROM ON HIGH.

But ye shall receive power, after that the Holy Ghost is come upon you: and ye shall be witnesses unto me both in Jerusalem, and in all Judaea, and in Samaria, and unto the uttermost part of the earth. (Acts 1:8)

Notice, the Word of God says that you *"shall receive power,"* not you "shall speak in tongues."

Five times in the book of Acts, the "tongue experience" is mentioned; in three of these times people spoke in tongues after being endued with power from on high. If three times they spoke in tongues after receiving power from on high and two times they may

80

not have spoken in tongues after receiving power from on high, this alone may discredit the statement that speaking in tongues is the initial and only evidence of being filled with the Holy Spirit.

I do not dispute, however, the teaching of tongues; several times in Scripture tongues are given as evidence of the Holy Spirit's filling. First and foremost, though, we must remember that endowment with power is the true mark of the Holy Spirit.

OTHER TONGUES

The Bible talks about two types of tongues: 1) other tongues or diversity of tongues and 2) unknown tongues or tongues of angels.

The gift of *other* tongues, which first took place at Pentecost, is the speaking of foreign languages by someone who has not been trained in that language. At Pentecost, it served as an experience for winning Jews to God.

> *And when the day of Pentecost was fully come, they were all with one accord in one place. And suddenly there came a sound from heaven as of a rushing mighty wind, and it filled all the house where they were sitting. And there appeared unto them cloven tongues like as of fire, and it sat upon each of them. And they were all filled with the Holy Ghost, and began to speak with **other** tongues, as the Spirit gave them the utterance.*
>
> (Acts 2:1–4, emphasis added)

Because this event at Pentecost is sometimes mistaken as the initial evidence of the baptism of the Holy Spirit, people who do not manifest tongues are often accused of not having this baptism. Remember, though, the universal evidence of the baptism of the Holy Spirit is power, not primarily the ability to speak in tongues. A look at the sequence of events in Acts clarifies this fact. Here's how: Acts 1:8 says that the initial evidence of this baptism is the power to be a witness unto Jesus Christ. All believers, through the baptism of the Holy Spirit, shall be His witnesses, having the power necessary for properly communicating Jesus to the world around them.

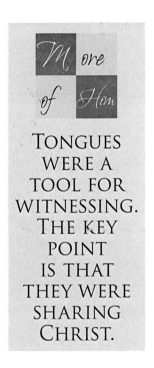

TONGUES WERE A TOOL FOR WITNESSING. THE KEY POINT IS THAT THEY WERE SHARING CHRIST.

But ye shall receive power, after that the Holy Ghost is come upon you: and ye shall be witnesses unto me both in Jerusalem, and in all Judaea, and in Samaria, and unto the uttermost part of the earth. (Acts 1:8)

Here Jesus' emphasis is on the witnessing, not on speaking in tongues. Acts 2:4, which records events happening after Acts 1:8, says that they *"began to speak with other tongues, as the Spirit gave them utterance."* In other words, they began speaking in tongues after the Spirit enabled them, or gave them the utterance. The key point, though, is that they were sharing Jesus; the

tongues were a tool for this witnessing. As they began to speak, men heard the wonderful works of God, and five thousand were added to the church.

Whenever there is an endowment of the Holy Spirit, the next step is sharing with someone the wonderful works of God through witnessing. Scripture is clear: The initial evidence of the baptism of the Holy Spirit is the ability to witness and reveal to others God's magnificent power. When Jesus asked Peter, *"Whom say ye that I am?"* (see Matthew 16:15; Mark 8:29; Luke 9:20), Peter answered, *"Thou art the Christ, the Son of the living God"* (Matthew 16:16). Jesus then commended Peter because He knew Peter did not receive this revelation through his own intuitive knowledge; He assured Peter that it was revealed to him by the Father: *"Blessed art thou, Simon Barjona: for flesh and blood hath not revealed it unto thee, but my Father which is in heaven"* (Matthew 16:17).

THE EXPERIENCE OF A LIFETIME

During a crusade in Tanzania, Africa, I was privileged to experience the gift of tongues for about four solid minutes. During this time I began speaking in tongues and praying in the Spirit until I suddenly realized there was a great commotion in the audience.

The open field where we were holding the crusade contained about sixty to seventy thousand Tanzanians who had come to hear the message. Some had walked for six weeks to get to the field where I would preach the Word for eight nights straight. After my anointing began to lift, I stood before the people and began singing a song. I noticed there were thousands of people moving toward the front of the platform. Since I wasn't familiar with the type of services the Tanzanians were accustomed to, I asked my interpreter what was going on. He immediately told me that I had delivered a complete salvation message to these people of Tanzania, entirely in their native language. I, of course, did not know the native language of the Tanzanians; I know without a doubt that this was a divine orchestration of the Lord Jesus Christ.

This was one of the most powerful experiences of my ministerial career, not because of any great thing I had done but because of the awesome and miraculous power of the Holy Spirit who carried out such an incredible feat. What a great honor it is to be used by the Lord!

UNKNOWN TONGUES

In addition to *other tongues*, we want to deal with *unknown tongues*.

> *For he that speaketh in an unknown tongue speaketh not unto men, but unto God: for no man understandeth him; howbeit in the spirit he speaketh mysteries.* (1 Corinthians 14:2)

The Bible also refers to these as *"the tongues...of angels."*

> *Though I speak with the tongues of men and of angels, and have not charity, I am become as sounding brass, or a tinkling cymbal.*
> (1 Corinthians 13:1)

"The tongues of men" that Paul mentioned here are the various languages that he spoke, such as Greek, Roman, and Hebrew. When he referred to *"the tongues...of angels,"* though, he was not talking about the other tongues or diversity of tongues from 1 Corinthians 14:11. He was referring instead to unknown tongues.

When I pray in an unknown tongue, *"my spirit prayeth, but my understanding is unfruitful"* (1 Corinthians 14:14). These are the tongues used to unravel prophecy, the tongues used to pray in the expressed will of God, and the tongues used by the Holy Spirit to pray through us and articulate the language of heaven so that our needs are met. One must understand that the language of heaven is not French; nor is it Chinese, Spanish, English, Hebrew, or Greek. The language of heaven is a language unto itself. It can be spoken only through the supernatural phenomenon of the Holy Spirit. And when it's spoken, a supernatural manifestation is released. This is where God, without human intellectual assistance, gives us the power to pray in the will of the Father.

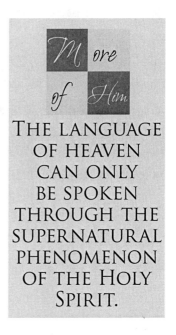

THE LANGUAGE OF HEAVEN CAN ONLY BE SPOKEN THROUGH THE SUPERNATURAL PHENOMENON OF THE HOLY SPIRIT.

Howbeit when he, the Spirit of truth, is come, he will guide you into all truth: for he shall not speak of himself; but whatsoever he shall hear, that shall he speak: and he will show you things to come. (John 16:13)

As Jesus said here, the Spirit speaks to us in a heavenly tongue. This is above and beyond the reasoning of men.

TONGUES ARE GOOD FOR YOU

Now that you know what really happened on the Day of Pentecost, you need to know that Pentecost is still happening today.

James wrote, *"Every good gift and every perfect gift is from above, and cometh down from the Father of lights, with whom is no variableness, neither shadow of turning"* (James 1:17). Because God is good and does not change, we can conclude that His gift of tongues is for today as well as for yesterday. Tongues, like *"every good…and… perfect gift,"* are still very good. They provide us with understanding, edification, a tool for praising God, and a sign of God's presence.

UNDERSTANDING: IT IS GOOD TO KNOW

Tongues are good because of the spiritual revelation they can provide to the Christian who seeks to know God intimately:

For he that speaketh in an unknown tongue speaketh not unto men, but unto God: for no

man understandeth him; howbeit in the spirit he speaketh mysteries. (1 Corinthians 14:2)

This word *"mysteries"* actually means "mouth-guarded, or concealed." So tongues are good because, whenever the language of the Holy Spirit is spoken, His mysteries are revealed so that we can better understand His ways.

Later in this chapter, Paul added that when we pray in an unknown tongue, "[our] *spirit prayeth, but* [our] *understanding is unfruitful*" (v. 14). In other words, Paul said that praying in tongues is good because the spirit prays—and if anybody knows what to say, the Spirit in us certainly does.

AS WE TUNE IN TO THE SPIRIT'S VOICE, WE WILL GROW IN WISDOM AND KNOWLEDGE OF GOD.

Paul encouraged us to pray so that we may hear the mysteries the Spirit speaks—and also interpret them. I would personally not want to speak a blessing in another language without understanding what that blessing was. If I was able to interpret it, though, I would be excited and edified. The experience of speaking in tongues is therefore nothing to be afraid of; we should not run from it or refuse to talk about it. Paul encouraged us to pray in both our known languages and in the Spirit's language. As we tune in to the Spirit's voice and cultivate our understanding, we will grow in wisdom and knowledge of God. And this is good.

> *What is it then? I will pray with the spirit, and I will pray with the understanding also: I will sing with the spirit, and I will sing with the understanding also.* (verse 15)

EDIFICATION: IT IS GOOD TO GROW

Paul said in 1 Corinthians 14:4, *"He that speaketh in an unknown tongue edifieth himself."* This word, *edify,* means "to build up." So tongues are also good because

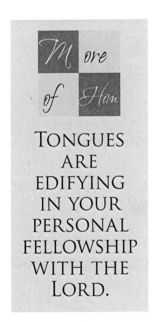

TONGUES ARE EDIFYING IN YOUR PERSONAL FELLOWSHIP WITH THE LORD.

they build up, or strengthen, our Christian experience. True, the gift is not for the building up of the church unless an interpretation is provided. But even when there is no interpretation, tongues are edifying in your personal fellowship with the Lord. When you pray in tongues privately, you are building up yourself, edifying your spirit—and that can only be good.

Paul's lengthy teaching in 1 Corinthians 14 was necessary because the Corinthians were so excited about their gift that they were constantly speaking out in tongues in public without interpretation. This was causing confusion, and Paul had to set them in order. When interpretation is provided for a public speaking of tongues, the entire body can be edified.

TOOL FOR PRAISE: IT IS GOOD TO WORSHIP THE LORD

The gift of tongues is also good because it gives us the freedom and ability to more adequately praise God. Once again, though, Paul cautioned about the need for order when worshipping in a congregational setting because of the potential of confusing others who can't enter in:

> *Else when thou shalt bless with the spirit, how shall he that occupieth the room of the unlearned say Amen at thy giving of thanks, seeing he understandeth not what thou sayest? For thou verily givest thanks well, but the other is not edified.*
>
> (1 Corinthians 14:16–17)

To help maintain order during times of public worship, Paul laid down God's guidelines for the use of tongues for praise:

> *I thank my God, I speak with tongues more than ye all: yet in the church I had rather speak five words with my understanding, that by my voice I might teach others also, than ten thousand words in an unknown tongue....How is it then, brethren? when ye come together, every one of you hath a psalm, hath a doctrine, hath a tongue, hath a revelation, hath an interpretation. Let all things be done unto edifying. If any man speak in an unknown tongue, let it be by two, or at the most by three, and that by course; and let one interpret. But if there be no interpreter, let him keep*

silence in the church; and let him speak to him-self, and to God. Let the prophets speak two or three, and let the other judge. If any thing be revealed to another that sitteth by, let the first hold his peace. For ye may all prophesy one by one, that all may learn, and all may be comforted. And the spirits of the prophets are subject to the prophets. For God is not the author of confusion, but of peace, as in all churches of the saints.
(1 Corinthians 14:18–19, 26–33)

God intended tongues as a spiritual gift to assist in praising Him; as this passage points out, though, we must always use the gifts in an orderly fashion.

SIGN OF GOD: IT IS GOOD TO SEE THE LORD

Tongues are also good because of the supernatural sign they provide; they point unbelievers to the reality of God. We see this throughout Scripture; occurrences of tongues mentioned in Acts include Pentecost, the first Gentile outpouring in Acts 10, and Paul's ministry to the Ephesian men in Acts 19.

Putting these three events together, we first see that God gave tongues as a sign to the unsaved Jews in Jerusalem to confirm the message of the apostles. At the home of the Roman centurion, Cornelius, we see that tongues served as a sign to the Jews gathered, showing them that non-Jews could be saved. And then we see tongues manifested in the distant regions of Asia Minor for the personal edification and spiritual benefit of the speakers themselves. And all this was good.

Paul's ministry to the followers of John the Baptist in Ephesus also showed the importance of the baptism of the Holy Spirit. This should serve as a witness to many denominations today that say speaking in tongues has passed away. Many congregations preach, "Just believe." Receiving after believing, however, is really the key, as these passages in Acts show us. If there are any pastors reading this who have resisted teaching the reality of the Holy Spirit's gift, start telling your congregation about the Holy Spirit and about how important it is to be filled with Him. He just might make tongues a sign to the unbelievers in your midst!

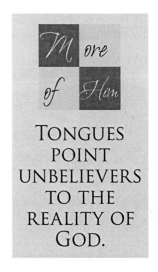

TONGUES POINT UNBELIEVERS TO THE REALITY OF GOD.

SPEAKING IN TONGUES IS NOT THE "SUPER-SAINT" GIFT

I would that ye all spake with tongues, but rather that ye prophesied: for greater is he that prophesieth than he that speaketh with tongues, except he interpret, that the church may receive edifying. (1 Corinthians 14:5)

In our discussion on tongues, we need to address a common misconception. Although tongues are good, their use or nonuse is certainly no measure of the spiritual superiority or inferiority of God's people in the church. In 1 Corinthians 14:5, Paul essentially said, "It is good that you can speak in tongues, but you aren't a super-saint because of it; you aren't spiritually superior or special because you have the gift of tongues." He went on to say that, unless an interpreter is present whenever a message is publicly spoken in tongues, the one who prophesies is greater than the one who speaks in tongues unless the message being interpreted.

People need to allow the gift of prophecy to work in them for the building up of the church. And, as I pointed out earlier in our discussion of the Day of Pentecost, this gift includes life-changing preaching.

Chapter Five

RECEIVING THE GIFT

Chapter Five

RECEIVING THE GIFT

efore we consider the question of how to receive the Holy Spirit, let's take one more look at the practice of tongues, because the church has been confused on this issue for many years. Some ministers have taught false doctrines concerning tongues, sometimes going so far as to say that those who don't speak in tongues will go to hell. Such people believe that speaking in tongues is a salvation commandment from the Lord, and they actually scare people into believing their theory. Such teaching, however, is totally false; it is a lie from the devil.

TONGUES: A GIFT—NOT A COMMAND

Once again, let's go to Paul for further truth on the subject of tongues, a topic that can be divisive if we do not have God's Word as the basis for our beliefs and doctrinal positions. Paul started his teaching on the Holy Spirit's gifts in 1 Corinthians 12:1: *"Now concerning spiritual gifts, brethren, I would not have you ignorant."* Paul took away our ignorance by telling us exactly what the spiritual gifts are:

> *But the manifestation of the Spirit is given to every man to profit withal. For to one is given by the Spirit the word of wisdom; to another the word of knowledge by the same Spirit; to another faith by the same Spirit; to another the gifts of healing by the same Spirit; to another the working of miracles; to another prophecy; to another discerning of spirits; to another divers kinds of tongues; to another the interpretation of tongues: but all these worketh that one and the selfsame Spirit, dividing to every man severally as he will.*
>
> (1 Corinthians 12:7–11)

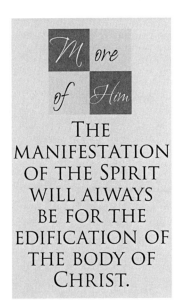

THE MANIFESTATION OF THE SPIRIT WILL ALWAYS BE FOR THE EDIFICATION OF THE BODY OF CHRIST.

Notice what Paul said: Not everybody is given the same gift. The Holy Spirit distributes the gifts as He chooses, giving to each person his or her own unique set of gifts. One thing is always certain, though: The manifestation of gifts of the Spirit are for the edification of the body of Christ. We are commanded to *"desire spiritual gifts"* (1 Corinthians 14:1). In other words, it's not our job to seek after particular gifts; the Holy Spirit makes that decision. He decides who gets what. Our job is simply to *"desire."*

Now look at the following passage from 1 Corinthians 12:

> *Now ye are the body of Christ, and members in particular. And God hath set some in the church, first apostles, secondarily prophets, thirdly teachers, after that miracles, then gifts of healings, helps, governments, diversities of tongues. Are all apostles? are all prophets? are all teachers? are all workers of miracles? Have all the gifts of healing? do all speak with tongues? do all interpret?*
> (1 Corinthians 12:27–30)

In this passage, which speaks about public, congregational gifts, Paul emphasized the fact that God has set certain public ministries within the church. Note again, though, that everybody does not have the same gift; the Spirit gives the gift of healings to one person, the gift of tongues to another, and the gift of miracles to yet another. Every member will not be given every gift. So if your theory says that everybody must speak in tongues when the church assembles—or even that there *must* be a message in tongues every time the church assembles—then you have missed the meaning of Paul's teaching here. The Spirit manifests Himself through various gifts, *as He wills.*

So not everyone will receive the gift of tongues. Scripture is clear, though, that we are all to desire the Spirit and His gifts, whatever He chooses them to be. Remember Paul's words: *"Even so ye, forasmuch as ye are zealous of spiritual gifts, seek that ye may excel to the edifying of the church"* (1 Corinthians 14:12).

Now why did Paul teach the church to be zealous of spiritual gifts if the Holy Spirit distributes the gifts as He chooses? Because He opens the door to those who knock, ask, and seek—remember? And the Holy Spirit wants to give gifts—the gifts that He determines—to those who eagerly desire them. Paul continued by instructing the church to be people of prayer, both in tongues and in human language, thus giving the Spirit freedom to edify the church:

THE HOLY SPIRIT WANTS TO GIVE GIFTS TO THOSE WHO EAGERLY DESIRE THEM.

For if I pray in an unknown tongue, my spirit prayeth, but my understanding is unfruitful. What is it then? I will pray with the spirit, and I will pray with the understanding also: I will sing with the spirit, and I will sing with the understanding also. Else when thou shalt bless with the spirit, how shall he that occupieth the room of the unlearned say Amen at thy giving of thanks, seeing he understandeth not what thou sayest? For thou verily givest thanks well, but the other is not edified. (1 Corinthians 14:14–17)

As we see from these Scriptures, the Spirit gives to certain ones the congregational gift of diversity of tongues; He commands no one to have it, however. What *is* commanded is repentance, water baptism in the name of the Lord, and filling with the Holy Spirit. (See Acts 2:38; 10:48; 17:30.) And uniting all of these is love. (See John

13:34; 1 John 4:7.) We'll talk more about love in the next chapter.

HOW TO RECEIVE

Now let's look into the realities of receiving the Holy Spirit and clear up some of the confusing doctrines that have kept many from experiencing His fullness. Many formulas and rituals have clouded and confounded the simple act of inviting the Holy Spirit into our hearts. He is waiting for us to respond to His call by repenting of our sins and receiving Him into our lives. Receiving Him doesn't have to be a complex process.

> *Then Peter said unto them, Repent, and be baptized every one of you in the name of Jesus Christ for the remission of sins, and ye shall receive the gift of the Holy Ghost. For the promise is unto you, and to your children, and to all that are afar off, even as many as the Lord our God shall call.*
> (Acts 2:38–39)

> *For every one that asketh receiveth; and he that seeketh findeth; and to him that knocketh it shall be opened. Or what man is there of you, whom if his son ask bread, will he give him a stone? Or if he ask a fish, will he give him a serpent? If ye then, being evil, know how to give good gifts unto your children, how much more shall your Father which is in heaven give good things to them that ask him?* (Matthew 7:8–11)

To *receive* something is "to take it into one's possession." When someone gives you a gift, do you respond by denying it? No, you take it. You receive it. And you're glad about receiving it. And when you receive that gift, it immediately becomes your possession. Why? Because it has been given to you.

In the same way, after you have accepted Christ as your Savior, you don't have to tarry or wait to be baptized with the Holy Spirit—God's gift from above. As Peter preached in Acts 2:39, *"The promise is unto you, and to your children, and to all that are afar off, even as many as the Lord our God shall call."* God has called all those who will to receive His gift. So why wait to receive it into your possession?

As a young Christian from the streets of Brooklyn, New York, I was excited about my new life, enthusiastic and ready to receive all that the Lord had promised me as an inheritance. Soon after giving my life to the Lord, I was filled with the Holy Spirit, which, along with the Word of God, liberated me from a life of drug abuse, oppression, and bondage. It wasn't tarrying at the altar or the laying on of hands that filled me with the Spirit and set me free; it was simply faith, asking to receive what God had promised.

NO NEED TO TARRY!

The devil wants you to wait, to tarry, so he can continue to drive you crazy. He wants you to remain without the Spirit as long as possible so you won't have the power to defeat him. We don't need to tarry, though; we need simply to receive. Tell the devil that you're going to have a receiving service—not a tarrying service—to accept and possess God's gift!

I want what God has promised to me, don't you? I need power, joy, love, faith, and meekness, and I need them right now to do God's work. This is the very reason the devil doesn't want us to have them. He has confused this issue more than any other simply to keep men enslaved and to hinder God's work. If you have been bound by the devil's lies on this issue, it is time to shake free from his weak chains in the name of Jesus! It is time to repent, to get cleaned up in your spirit, and to receive God's gift of power and love. Now is the time to be baptized in water and receive the Holy Spirit. There's no need to tarry or wait.

More of Him

I NEED POWER, JOY, LOVE, FAITH, AND MEEKNESS IN ORDER TO DO GOD'S WORK, AND I NEED THEM NOW.

Now, I'm not suggesting that God gives us everything we want simply for the asking. He doesn't work on a "name-it-claim-it" basis. What I am suggesting, though, is that we can be confident about receiving those things that God's Word has promised us. To those who believe on His name for salvation, He has already assured the gift of Holy Spirit baptism. As such, we can be confident that, in God's time, the Spirit's working will be evident in our lives.

"How do I receive His promised gift?" you ask. You receive it by humbly but boldly asking for it. You have to do the asking, the seeking, and the knocking. If your earthly father told you a wonderful new gift had been purchased for you—and that it was ready and waiting, all you had to do was ask—you would be confident in asking for it. You would say, "Dad, may I please have that gift?" In the same way, the gift of the Holy Spirit was made available to all Christians—but the asking must take place.

> *Ask, and it shall be given you; seek, and ye shall find; knock, and it shall be opened unto you: for every one that asketh receiveth; and he that seeketh findeth; and to him that knocketh it shall be opened.* (Matthew 7:7–8)

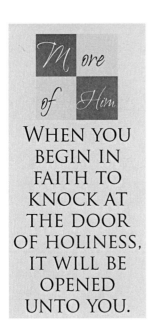

WHEN YOU BEGIN IN FAITH TO KNOCK AT THE DOOR OF HOLINESS, IT WILL BE OPENED UNTO YOU.

When you were out of the will of God, you spent more than enough time asking and seeking for the wrong things. Now is the time to ask for the good things of God, so you can do His work and live an overcomer's life. Happiness, strength, good health, prosperity, and power over the enemy can be found in Jesus. When you begin in faith to knock at the door to seek, it will be opened unto you. When you ask the One who has all power to give you this gift of the Holy Spirit, He will answer your request.

> *For every one that asketh receiveth; and he that seeketh findeth; and to him that knocketh it shall*

be opened. If a son shall ask bread of any of you that is a father, will he give him a stone? or if he ask a fish, will he for a fish give him a serpent? Or if he shall ask an egg, will he offer him a scorpion? If ye then, being evil, know how to give good gifts unto your children: how much more shall your heavenly Father give the Holy Spirit to them that ask him? (Luke 11:10–13)

In this passage, Jesus proved that "asking"—not "tarrying"—is the key to receiving the Holy Spirit. When you seek to find the door to God's New Testament promise of the Spirit, asking will unlock it. Once you're inside the door and the Giver has handed you the gift, it's your job to take it and move along in the power that has been given to you.

Perhaps one reason the disciples had to tarry in the book of Acts was because the Holy Spirit was making His debut. The promised baptism, or "clothing" of His power was promised by our resurrected Lord just before His ascension in Luke 24:49: *"Tarry ye in the city of Jerusalem, until ye be endued with power from on high."* He would come according to God's calendar, on the harvest festival

More of Him

"ASKING"— NOT "TARRYING"— IS THE KEY TO RECEIVING THE HOLY SPIRIT.

Day of Pentecost as directed by God. But now that He has come, those who experience the Passover by accepting Jesus Christ, God's Passover Lamb, can receive the baptism of the Holy Spirit by simply asking in faith.

NO CHEERLEADING NEEDED!

The process is very simple indeed: We must only seek, knock, and ask; then the fullness of the Spirit will be given. But many people make it seem so difficult. Some teach that if you wait long enough, pray hard enough, scream loud enough, or say, "Thank You, Jesus—thank You, Jesus—thank You, Jesus," fast enough, you will receive the Holy Spirit. These techniques are equally unscriptural.

Scripture doesn't teach that Jesus' followers must get into prayer lines or create ritualistic pandemonium. The gift of the Spirit does not have to be conjured up or invoked as in some type of mystical séance. Those types of practices are man-made, and God isn't pleased with them. The Holy Spirit doesn't need a cheerleader to help Him out or to invoke His power; He can fill us with His presence without our help. All we need to do is repent and receive Jesus, be baptized in His name, and receive the Holy Spirit.

THE KEY TO RECEIVING: HUNGER AND THIRST

Desire is where it starts. Jesus said, *"Blessed are they which do hunger and thirst after righteousness: for they shall be filled"* (Matthew 5:6). There are two words you have to notice here: *"hunger"* and *"thirst."* These words imply a desire, a longing, a want, or a need. God gives to those who want what He has. He gives to those who do whatever it takes to receive the Holy Spirit. And this, in its simplest terms, is what constitutes faith.

> *But without faith it is impossible to please him: for he that cometh to God must believe that he is, and that he is a rewarder of them that diligently seek him.* (Hebrews 11:6)

Being hungry or thirsty implies that you need fulfillment, which causes you to come to God, believe that He is the Baptizer in the Holy Spirit, ask for the Holy Spirit, and receive the gift of His indwelling presence. Simple! God wants you to ask Him so that He can give. *"But my God shall supply all your need according to his riches in glory by Christ Jesus"* (Philippians 4:19).

God won't let your wants and needs go unattended, especially when your desire is to be more like Him. All you need to do is ask and receive, and He will bless your soul.

When I was filled with the Holy Spirit, not only was my newfound liberation in Christ less than acceptable through the eyes of my church, but I was considered to be in outright rebellion to the teaching set forth by the leaders. This was because of how I had received the Holy Spirit, which ultimately placed the authenticity of my gift on trial. In the end, my gift would be accepted by the congregation only if it was authenticated by man (blessed and certified by one of our elders) during a tarrying service at my church.

Needless to say, however, I had already been filled with the Holy Spirit days before in my bedroom at home. The Spirit of the Lord overwhelmed me, and as I began speaking in tongues, my mother, who was a Seventh-day Adventist, stood pounding on the other side of the door, demanding that I "Shut up all that noise!" So it wasn't through the laying on of hands or through a tarrying service that God ushered the Holy Spirit into my life; it was my faith, my desire, my hungering and thirsting that got His atten tion. That is why it's important for a person not just to know *about* Jesus, but to know Him in an intimate, personal way. It is only then that the Lord will develop in your life the real evidence of the Spirit, which is love.

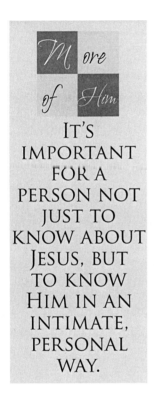

IT'S IMPORTANT FOR A PERSON NOT JUST TO KNOW ABOUT JESUS, BUT TO KNOW HIM IN AN INTIMATE, PERSONAL WAY.

If tarrying or the laying on of hands was your means for receiving the Holy Spirit, then you should not allow anyone, including me, to dispute the authenticity of your gift. Many have, in times past, received the Spirit's indwelling through both methods. But for others, such as myself, the method of simply asking and receiving is appropriate. It should neither be disputed nor belittled; instead it should be looked upon as a method that is in accordance with the Word of God.

RECEIVING THE *Gift*

GOD KEEPS HIS PROMISES

Then Peter said unto them, Repent, and be baptized every one of you in the name of Jesus Christ for the remission of sins, and ye shall receive the gift of the Holy Ghost. For the promise is unto you, and to your children, and to all that are afar off, even as many as the Lord our God shall call.
(Acts 2:38–39)

The Holy Spirit baptism is not a conjured-up religious façade but a promised gift from the Father to His children. If your natural father knocked on your door holding the keys to a brand new car, would you shun him and reject the gift? Would you tell him, "No, thank you. I'm satisfied just walking around. I don't need a car right now"? Of course not! Instead, you'd receive the gift with gladness. Likewise, we should exercise that same enthusiasm in receiving a wonderful gift from the greatest Father of all—the gift of the Holy Spirit. Why walk when you can ride on His cloud of glory as He leads you on the best path for reaching your divine destiny?

The strategy of Lucifer, however, is to make you believe that receiving this gift of the Holy Spirit is of little or no significance. He would also have you believe that you must go through a long, drawn-out ritual. But the truth is, receiving this blessing *is* a very significant part of the Christian experience, and the only prerequisite for receiving the gift is salvation. One needs only to ask and have faith to receive.

Remember, the Spirit of God not only guides; He also changes us from the inside out. I often question those who claim to be filled but never change their character or the way they treat others. Such people never experience victory but remain in a constant state of depression and oppression. When you receive this precious gift into your life, He is quickened any time you're tempted to engage in ungodly acts or behaviors. He supplies you with the fruit of the Spirit and the ability to draw strength in those times of weakness. No, the Holy Spirit is not a guarantee that life will be free of problems and temptations or that there will never be times of weakness. But with the Holy Spirit there will come guidance, warnings of oncoming danger, and peace in the midst of trials.

> THE HOLY SPIRIT SUPPLIES YOU WITH THE FRUIT OF THE SPIRIT AND THE ABILITY TO DRAW STRENGTH FROM THE FATHER IN TIMES OF WEAKNESS.

But the fruit of the Spirit is love, joy, peace, long-suffering, gentleness, goodness, faith, meekness, temperance: against such there is no law. And they that are Christ's have crucified the flesh with the affections and lusts. If we live in the Spirit, let us also walk in the Spirit. Let us not be desirous of vain glory, provoking one another, envying one another. (Galatians 5:22–26)

Ask the One who has all power to fill you with His Spirit. Then His love, joy, and freedom will replace hate, depression, and oppression; His peace will remove anxiety; His gentleness and goodness will overcome envy and strife; and His presence will turn disbelief into strong faith. Ask Him now so that you may come to experience the knowledge of His infinite wisdom and power.

Chapter Six

IT ALL COMES DOWN TO
LOVE AND ORDER

Chapter Six

IT ALL COMES DOWN TO LOVE AND ORDER

To understand the real evidence of God's Holy Spirit, we must refer once more to Paul's first letter to the Corinthians:

Though I speak with the tongues of men and of angels, and have not charity, I am become as sounding brass, or a tinkling cymbal. And though I have the gift of prophecy, and understand all mysteries, and all knowledge; and though I have all faith, so that I could remove mountains, and have not charity, I am nothing.

(1 Corinthians 13:1–2)

Here Paul clearly named the fruit, or evidence, of the Spirit: love. Wouldn't you know it; right in the middle of this passage on spiritual gifts—including tongues—Scripture reminds us that love, not spiritual gifts, is the touchstone of the Spirit's indwelling! The Bible says that a tree is known by the fruit it bears. And the fruit, or evidence, of the Spirit is love. *"But the fruit of the Spirit is love, joy, peace, longsuffering, gentleness, goodness, faith, meekness, temperance: against such there is no law"* (Galatians 5:22–23).

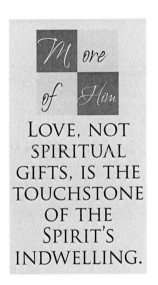

LOVE, NOT SPIRITUAL GIFTS, IS THE TOUCHSTONE OF THE SPIRIT'S INDWELLING.

Now if the gift of tongues was a fruit of the Spirit or evidence of His presence, it would have been listed here with the other fruits in Paul's definitive list. But it wasn't; instead, it was listed elsewhere in Scripture among the gifts of the Spirit.

Even though the Bible emphasizes tongues, it puts so much more emphasis on love. Paul's first letter to the Corinthians straightforwardly reminds us that everything, even the Spirit's gifts, are meaningless without love.

Though I speak with the tongues of men and of angels, and have not charity [love], I am become as sounding brass, or a tinkling cymbal. And though I have the gift of prophecy, and understand all mysteries, and all knowledge; and though I have all faith, so that I could remove mountains, and have not charity [love], I am nothing.

(1 Corinthians 13:1–2)

Notice that Paul named both of the Holy Spirit's speaking gifts—tongues and prophecy—along with knowledge and faith in this passage. He said you can have and use all those gifts—but if you don't have love, it doesn't profit you one bit!

So love is the *fruit* of the Spirit in our lives, not tongues, is the evidence that we are Christ's. Yet too many in our churches have focused on the gifts of the Spirit instead of His fruit. The apostle John wrote,

> *We know that we have passed from death unto life, because we love the brethren. He that loveth not his brother abideth in death.*   (1 John 3:14)

In other words, you can speak in tongues all you want; if you don't love, though, you still abide in death. If you harbor hate in your heart, it doesn't matter how much you speak in tongues. *"Whosoever hateth his brother is a murderer: and ye know that no murderer hath eternal life abiding in him"* (v. 15). Love is the evidence of the Spirit.

IS THE EVIDENCE PRESENT IN YOUR LIFE?

Examine your own life. Is the evidence of the Spirit present? Consider John's first epistle and the evidence of being filled with the Spirit that he described there:

> *Beloved, let us love one another: for love is of God; and every one that loveth is born of God, and knoweth God. He that loveth not knoweth not God; for God is love.*   (1 John 4:7–8)

> *No man hath seen God at any time. If we love one another, God dwelleth in us, and his love is*

perfected in us. Hereby know we that we dwell in him, and he in us, because he hath given us of his Spirit. (1 John 4:12–13)

If a man say, I love God, and hateth his brother, he is a liar: for he that loveth not his brother whom he hath seen, how can he love God whom he hath not seen? And this commandment have we from him, That he who loveth God love his brother also. (verses 20–21)

Just as Paul emphasized the importance of love in his letters, so did John. John's works as a leader in the early church, as well as the works of the other apostles, were done in love. When they received the Holy Spirit, they received the love of God. This in turn led them to think of others' needs before their own. They were empowered with the Holy Spirit's love to fulfill Christ's teaching recorded in Matthew 25:35–36:

For I was an hungered, and ye gave me meat: I was thirsty, and ye gave me drink: I was a stranger, and ye took me in: naked, and ye clothed me: I was sick, and ye visited me: I was in prison, and ye came unto me.

If you have accepted Christ's gift of salvation, then this love is in your heart as well:

And hope maketh not ashamed; because the love of God is shed abroad in our hearts by the Holy Ghost which is given unto us. (Romans 5:5)

Sometimes love will lead you to sacrifice so that someone else can be helped. When you give to others without complaining or telling everyone that you gave, this is the love of God working in your life. And love extends beyond just our family and friends. When you are compassionate toward someone else's grandparents and visit them in the hospital, the love of God is working in your life. When it's not your child in prison but someone else's whom you visit, this is the love of God working in your life. If you are a preacher and you go anywhere to preach the gospel for free, whether your own congregation is there or not, this is the love of God working in your life. And when you do all these things in secret, when you don't broadcast them but keep them between God and yourself, this is good; this is God's love.

More of Him

SOMETIMES LOVE WILL LEAD YOU TO SACRIFICE SO THAT SOMEONE ELSE CAN BE HELPED.

> *Charity suffereth long, and is kind; charity envieth not; charity vaunteth not itself, is not puffed up, doth not behave itself unseemly, seeketh not her own, is not easily provoked, thinketh no evil; rejoiceth not in iniquity, but rejoiceth in the truth; beareth all things, believeth all things, hopeth all things, endureth all things.*
>
> (1 Corinthians 13:4–7)

When you have the love of God, you can visibly see these characteristics of the Holy Spirit manifest in your life. Is such evidence present in your life? Do you love unconditionally? Do you show your love? We often say we love others, but do we really? Are we showing the fruit?

My little children, let us not love in word, neither in tongue; but in deed and in truth. (1 John 3:18)

DECENTLY AND IN ORDER

Let all things be done decently and in order.
(1 Corinthians 14:40)

Closely related to love is the issue of order. We've already talked about how spiritual gifts, even the gift of tongues, mean nothing if the Spirit's fruit, or evidence, is absent. Similarly, spiritual gifts are no good unless we use them in the orderly fashion God has commanded. To use God's spiritual gifts in a disorderly way is both unloving toward our Christian brothers and sisters and disobedient toward God.

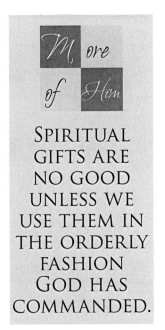

SPIRITUAL GIFTS ARE NO GOOD UNLESS WE USE THEM IN THE ORDERLY FASHION GOD HAS COMMANDED.

Let's turn again to Paul's first letter to the Corinthians for guidance on the use of tongues:

Now, brethren, if I come unto you speaking with tongues, what shall I profit you, except I shall speak to you either by revelation, or by knowledge, or by prophesying, or by doctrine? And even things without life giving sound, whether pipe or harp, except they give a

118

distinction in the sounds, how shall it be known what is piped or harped? For if the trumpet give an uncertain sound, who shall prepare himself to the battle? So likewise ye, except ye utter by the tongue words easy to be understood, how shall it be known what is spoken? for ye shall speak into the air. There are, it may be, so many kinds of voices in the world, and none of them is without signification. Therefore if I know not the meaning of the voice, I shall be unto him that speaketh a barbarian, and he that speaketh shall be a barbarian unto me....I thank my God, I speak with tongues more than ye all: yet in the church I had rather speak five words with my understanding, that by my voice I might teach others also, than ten thousand words in an unknown tongue.

(1 Corinthians 14:6–11, 18–19)

Here Paul addressed the "fleshly" problems the Corinthians were experiencing when they spoke in tongues. Notice that the same problem is present in many churches today. A lot of things are being done in the flesh instead of in the Spirit. Specifically, Paul said here that it doesn't make sense to get up in church and speak an unknown tongue to a congregation that can't understand a single word of it. This is an unloving and ungodly thing to do. It is more beneficial to edify and to help others than yourself. And when you speak in an unknown tongue, without an interpreter, others are not edified.

I believe that many in today's modern church have turned tongues into a "fad." They mistakenly believe it's popular to speak in an unknown tongue, even though the Holy Spirit may have nothing to do with it. These fad-seekers tend to think that speaking in tongues during church services will make them super-saints. This, however, is not scriptural. In fact, this mistaken belief was so widespread in Corinth that Paul devoted an entire chapter of 1 Corinthians to addressing it!

Don't get me wrong; Paul encouraged everyone to seek after the Spirit and receive the gift of tongues. But he also rebuked the church for its disorderly behavior and instructed its members to move only in God's spiritual order.

> *If therefore the whole church be come together into one place, and all speak with tongues, and there come in those that are unlearned, or unbelievers, will they not say that ye are mad? But if all prophesy, and there come in one that believeth not, or one unlearned, he is convinced of all, he is judged of all: and thus are the secrets of his heart made manifest; and so falling down on his face he will worship God, and report that God is in you of a truth.*
>
> (1 Corinthians 14:23–25)

In other words, Paul directed the Corinthian church to abstain from speaking in tongues in public without interpretation because of the confusion it could cause in the congregation. He did not condemn the use of public tongues; rather he instructed the Corinthian church on the importance of order, including the need for interpretation within a congregational use of tongues.

IT ALL COMES DOWN TO *Love and Order*

> *How is it then, brethren? when ye come together,*
> *every one of you hath a psalm, hath a doctrine, hath*
> *a tongue, hath a revelation, hath an interpretation.*
> *Let all things be done unto edifying. If any man*
> *speak in an unknown tongue, let it be by two, or at*
> *the most by three, and that by course; and let one*
> *interpret. But if there be no interpreter, let him keep*
> *silence in the church; and let him speak to himself,*
> *and to God. Let the prophets speak two or three,*
> *and let the other judge. If any thing be revealed to*
> *another that sitteth by, let the first hold his peace.*
> *For ye may all prophesy one by one, that all may*
> *learn, and all may be comforted. And the spirits of*
> *the prophets are subject to the prophets. For God is*
> *not the author of confusion, but of peace, as in all*
> *churches of the saints.* (1 Corinthians 14:26–33)

Paul, in essence, said, "Why is everyone flaunting his own abilities rather than edifying others and sharing the love of Christ through the power of God? Someone needs edifying; someone needs help. And he can't get it because a group of people are living in the flesh and acting in ways that are totally out of order!"

Notice that Paul didn't say, "Let twenty speak and five interpret." No, he said, *"If any man speak in an unknown tongue, let it be by two, or at the most by three, and that by course; and let one interpret."* He also added, *"But if there be no interpreter, let him keep silence in the church; and let him speak to himself, and to God."*

"But pastor, I can't control it," someone says. That's not true, and it doesn't matter; the Lord isn't going to contradict His Word.

I have often spoken to people who say to me, "I just can't help myself! I speak in tongues at my job, in the grocery store, and I never know when the Spirit is going to provoke me to start speaking. And when I start, sometimes I just can't stop."

Well, I beg to differ with the "I just can't help myself" philosophy. Satan's practice is always to take what God meant for a blessing and turn it into a curse. As a believer, you should always live as one who *encourages* others to come to Christ—not as one who *repels* them. Let us not ignore the instructions given in God's Word:

If therefore the whole church be come together into one place, and all speak with tongues, and there come in those that are unlearned, or unbelievers, will they not say that ye are mad? But if all prophesy, and there come in one that believeth not, or one unlearned, he is convinced of all, he is judged of all: and thus are the secrets of his heart made manifest; and so falling down on his face he will worship God, and report that God is in you of a truth. How is it then, brethren? when ye come together, every one of you hath a psalm, hath a doctrine, hath a tongue, hath a revelation, hath an interpretation. Let all things be done unto edifying. If any man speak in an unknown tongue, let it be by two, or at the most by three, and that by course; and let one interpret. But if there be no interpreter, let him keep silence in the church; and let him speak to himself, and to God. Let the prophets speak two or three, and let the other judge. If any thing be revealed to another that sitteth by,

let the first hold his peace. For ye may all proph-
esy one by one, that all may learn, and all may
be comforted. And the spirits of the prophets are
subject to the prophets. For God is not the author
of confusion, but of peace, as in all churches of the
saints. (1 Corinthians 14:23–33)

God is not one to send confusion. He is a God of peace and order. Whenever we lose focus, that which God has gifted to us as a blessing can become to us an unfortunate curse. God kept His promise by sending His Comforter; we must respond by keeping His Word, as well, by practicing to do *"all things...decently and in order"* (v. 40).

Being filled with the Holy Spirit is not a time for us as believers to flaunt our stuff and show the world how "holy" we are. Instead, it's a time to understand that it's not by our might, nor by our power, but by the Spirit of the Lord that we are able to be used for His glory. (See Zechariah 4:6.)

More of Him

IT'S NOT BY OUR MIGHT, NOR BY OUR POWER, BUT BY THE SPIRIT OF THE LORD THAT WE ARE ABLE TO BE USED FOR HIS GLORY.

I encourage everyone—pastors, Sunday school teachers, elders, husbands, wives, and children alike—to read this chapter very carefully before entering your sanctuary doors for another service. May the Holy Spirit convict you to keep His good order.

Chapter Seven

CONTROLLING JEZEBEL'S DECEPTION AND DECEIT

Chapter Seven

CONTROLLING JEZEBEL'S DECEPTION AND DECEIT

The technological age of the twenty-first century has exposed us to a world of options from which to choose when it comes to religion. With so many voices, opinions, and so-called facts to back up the various doctrines and beliefs that are now inundating our airwaves, talk shows, textbooks, and even many of our churches, thousands are unknowingly becoming bewitched by doctrines of devils, seducing spirits, and all manner of ungodliness that comes for one purpose—to kill, steal, and to destroy the authenticity of the Word of God. Satan realizes now more than ever that his time is short. Because of this fact, he has hastened his tactics, using any and every avenue possible to plant doubt and unbelief into the mind of the unbeliever and believer alike.

What is right and what is wrong? That seems to be the question of today among those who in times past left no room for doubt because they were filled with the Word of God that casts out all doubt and unbelief. Throughout centuries this same problem has had to be addressed among those who know Jesus as Lord.

> *Oh, foolish Galatians! What magician has cast an evil spell on you? For you used to see the meaning of Jesus Christ's death as clearly as though I had shown you a signboard with a picture of Christ dying on the cross.* (Galatians 3:1 NLT)

Paul likened the behavior of the Galatians to a spell that had been cast, which had blinded their spiritual vision, causing them to act out of the norm. These same people, who had once had such great faith in the person of the Lord Jesus Christ, were now trying to *"become perfect in their own human effort"* (verse 3). They were belittling the significance of the power of God that He'd willed to them through His death and resurrection. On a weekly basis, many sitting right in the church become victims of this same ploy. The devil plays with the vulnerabilities of the saints of God in an attempt to use our weaknesses against us. The more dependent we become upon our own human ingenuity and the less dependent we are upon the Word of God, the more pleased the devil becomes with our actions. He then sends voices to stroke our ego and to distract us from relying upon the power of God so that we crack the door to ungodly outside influences.

The Galatians once saw the meaning and significance of Christ's death as clearly as *"a signboard with a picture of Christ dying on the cross."* Somehow, however, they'd allowed themselves to become bewitched.

Many things can come to bewitch you and alter your way of thinking when it comes to the truth concerning the Word of God. When we hear the word *bewitch,* we often think of secret potions, séances, and dark rituals, when in fact, many of us are bewitched simply by the conversations that we allow ourselves to listen to on a daily basis. *Bewitched* simply means to be charmed or fascinated to the point that your resistance is weakened and you begin giving in to the ideas, philosophies, or the will of another person—a form of witchcraft.

The Galatians were misled into believing more in the works of their flesh than the significance of the power of God—this same power that had enabled them to come through such great sufferings of the past. This is why the Galatians had to be reminded from where the Lord had brought them in order to go forth with a renewed spirit, being led by the mind of Christ. You can become so complacent that you lose sight of your testimony and instead begin leaning on the finite boundaries of human ingenuity. It is at this stage that the enemy uses this erroneous way of thinking to open your mind to the doctrines of men that contradict and confuse your way of thinking against the teachings of

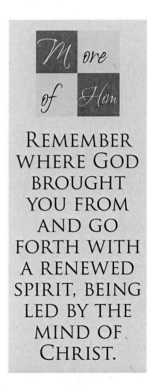

More of Him

REMEMBER WHERE GOD BROUGHT YOU FROM AND GO FORTH WITH A RENEWED SPIRIT, BEING LED BY THE MIND OF CHRIST.

the Word of God. You will find yourself thinking that there is a better way for you to conquer life's challenges, compromising what you know to be God's truth for the so-called logic of human ingenuity.

King Saul learned this lesson the hard way when the Lord instructed him in 1 Samuel chapter 15 to destroy the Amalekites and all that they have. Instead of obeying God, Saul began listening to the people and disobeyed God's command. Instead of following the Lord's instructions, Saul took it upon himself to spare *"Agag [the king], the best of the sheep, and of the oxen, and of the fatlings, and the lambs, and all that was good, and would not utterly destroy them: but everything that was vile and refuse, that they destroyed utterly"* (verse 9). When confronted by Samuel of the Lord's displeasure with his actions, Saul claimed to have saved the animals in order to offer them as a sacrifice to the Lord, but Samuel rebuked him,

> *Hath the Lord as great delight in burnt offerings and sacrifices as in obeying the voice of the Lord? Behold, to obey is better than sacrifice, and to hearken than the fat of rams. For rebellion is as the sin of witchcraft, and stubbornness is as iniquity and idolatry. Because thou hast rejected the word of the Lord, he hath also rejected thee from being king.* (1 Samuel 15:22–23)

Saul responded, *"I have sinned: for I have transgressed the commandment of the Lord, and thy words: because I feared the people, and obeyed their voice"* (verse 24).

Rebellion against what you know is the commandment of God is witchcraft. In your stubbornness, you idolize your own wants, needs, and desires above God. I'm sure that when God gave Saul the commandment, he probably had every intention of obeying God's Word. When he arrived in Amalek, however, and saw the richness of the land, he began to question whether or not God's way was the best plan of action. He became bewitched by his fear of people.

Think of the times when the Lord has given you a direct command. You shouted, gave praise to God, and even thanked Him for taking the time to speak to you, but when it came time to act upon what God had spoken, something happened to make you question the Word of the Lord. In hindsight, however, you realized the error of your ways, but by then it was too late.

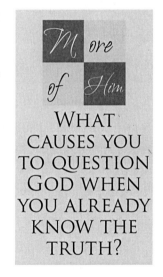

More of Him

WHAT CAUSES YOU TO QUESTION GOD WHEN YOU ALREADY KNOW THE TRUTH?

What is the source of your bewitching spell? What causes you to question God when you already know the truth? In other words, what has bewitched you? Is it your education, the voices of family and friends, greed, fear, loneliness? What causes you to disobey God and hold on to things that He has commanded you to destroy?

Many things can come to hinder your walk and test your faith in God. It is Satan's intention to use your own personal desires and/or weaknesses against you in order to keep you at a place where God is displeased with your actions. In your quest to succeed in life and

131

to accomplish your goals and aspirations, don't allow yourself to become bewitched by the subtle tactics of the devil. In God you can do all things, but without Him, you will be seduced into doing things your own way, and in the end you will surely fail.

> *Notwithstanding I have a few things against thee, because thou sufferest that woman Jezebel, which calleth herself a prophetess, to teach and to seduce my servants to commit fornication, and to eat things sacrificed unto idols.*
> (Revelation 2:20)

In the Old Testament, Jezebel was a living, breathing woman who did all manner of evil and seduced others into committing her same idolatrous acts. Today, Jezebel continues to live and reign but in the form of a spirit. She disguises herself as a gentle sheep, but underneath her fragile exterior lies a raving wolf, patiently waiting to devour anyone who takes the time to listen to her enticements. There are many warning signs to expose the Jezebel spirit in operation:

1. **It is Seducing.** The spirit of Jezebel comes as a gentle, helpful form of support whose desire is to assist you in meeting your goals and aspirations, but beware! There is always an ulterior motive behind their actions. And although we often refer to Jezebel as female, her spirit knows no gender. Both men and women can be used as her vehicle of choice in accomplishing her selfish and destructive goals.

2. **It is Controlling.** Jezebel gets you to believe that her way of doing things is the most sensible means of accomplishing what needs to be done. She gets you to block out all other voices so that she becomes the ruling force steering your decisions in life. In doing so she not only controls you, but is also able to use you to control others in a means to carry on her cycle of ungodliness, witchcraft, and rebellion. You become so tuned in to the voice and lies of Jezebel that it becomes impossible for you to see the truth, even when it's staring you right in face. Because you've been bewitched, you see those who are trying to get you back onto the right path as the enemy and those being used by the Jezebel spirit as your newfound saviors.

3. **It is Destructive.** Jezebel's ultimate purpose is total destruction. The book of 1 Kings shows her wreaking havoc and killing the prophets of God. Today the Jezebel spirit continues its quest of destruction upon the people of God. When she cannot succeed in controlling your way of thinking, she uses those who are under her spell to set out to destroy you.

Those who knew Jezebel, feared her. That was, until Elijah came onto the scene and challenged Jezebel and her prophets of Baal. Elijah boldly defied Jezebel's prophets and openly challenged them to a duel. First Kings 18 shows the false prophets of Jezebel and Elijah, the prophet of the Lord, both bringing a sacrifice to the altar. The god who consumed his sacrifice by fire would be the god that the people would serve. As the crowd waited in anticipation, the false prophets rent their clothes, cut themselves, and cried out tirelessly to Baal, but to no avail. Baal never showed up, and their sacrifice remained on their altar, regardless of their antics in calling upon their false god. Elijah then built an altar to God, soaked it with water, along with the sacrifice, and cried out to God. Not only was the sacrifice consumed, but even the water that stood in the trench around it was consumed by fire.

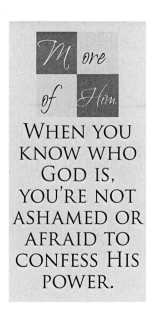

WHEN YOU KNOW WHO GOD IS, YOU'RE NOT ASHAMED OR AFRAID TO CONFESS HIS POWER.

When you know who your God is, you're not ashamed or afraid to confess His power. It's when defeat looks inevitable that God performs His greatest works. Elijah saw no need to force God upon any of the onlookers, but simply stated that He'd allow the outcome of this showdown to speak for itself:

> *And Elijah came unto all the people, and said, How long halt ye between two opinions? if the LORD be God, follow him: but if Baal, then follow him. And the people answered him not a word. Let them therefore give us two bullocks; and let them choose one bullock for themselves, and cut it in pieces, and lay it on wood, and put no fire*

under: and I will dress the other bullock, and lay it on wood, and put no fire under:....call ye on the name of your gods, and I will call on the name of the Lord: and the God that answereth by fire, let him be God. And all the people answered and said, It is well spoken. (1 Kings 18:21, 23–24)

When the Spirit of the Lord shows up, He destroys every yoke, including the witchcraft that accompanies the spirit of Jezebel. *"And when all the people saw it, they fell on their faces: and they said, The Lord, he is the God; the Lord, he is the God"* (verse 39). When the people saw how the Lord consumed Elijah's sacrifice and the water with fire, their fear of Jezebel and her false god Baal succumbed to the unde-niable power of God. By the com-mand of Elijah, they took hold of Jezebel's false prophets of Baal so that none of them could escape. When a person has fallen prey to the spiritual seduction of the Jezebel spirit, nothing can open his eyes of enlightenment quite like the power of God in operation. In the presence of God, the covers are snatched off of Jezebel's phony façade. As this spirit's real motives are unveiled, those who were under her spell awake out of their deep sleep of deception.

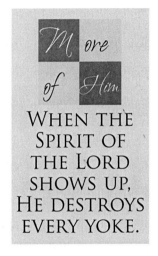

More of Him

WHEN THE SPIRIT OF THE LORD SHOWS UP, HE DESTROYS EVERY YOKE.

The Jezebel spirit is a destructive force that has unfortunately crept into many churches. Consequently, people within the walls of many of our religious institutions are finding themselves being led by familiar spirits, doctrines of devils, and seductive suggestions of enticement. The actions of the people are based upon fear and not upon their desire to please God. These controlling spirits are what hinder us from seeing the full manifestation of the power of God rain down as it did when Elijah called upon God to consume his sacrifice. When these spirits are broken, however, we see addicts freed from the claws of addiction, incurable diseases healed, minds renewed, and souls set free! Leadership that shows you the unmistakable power of God cannot be denied or duplicated. Those who are spiritual can spot a fake and are not easily swayed by the applause of the crowd.

The cloud of deception chokes the life out of the church but the power of God sends revival. The spirit of Jezebel is unrepentant. It stops at nothing, not even death, to accomplish its destructive goals. Jezebel, having her chance to repent, refused to do so. Instead, when her husband Ahab gave her the news concerning the plight of her prophets, it infuriated her even more.

And Ahab told Jezebel all that Elijah had done, and withal how he had slain all the prophets with the sword. Then Jezebel sent a messenger unto Elijah, saying, So let the gods do to me, and more also, if I make not thy life as the life of one of them by to morrow about this time. (1 Kings 19:1–2)

Persons driven by this spirit are intoxicated with having their way or no way at all. They will stop at nothing to achieve their ungodly agendas, even challenging you and the God you serve to feed their fury, jealousy, and rage. Still, you must remember that you're not dealing with an actual individual, but you're wrestling with the spirit that is driving this person to act in a manner that he or she might not otherwise behave void of the Jezebel spirit. *"For we wrestle not against flesh and blood, but against principalities, against powers, against the rulers of the darkness of this world, against spiritual wickedness in high places"* (Ephesians 6:12). The trick of the devil is to get you so infuriated with the individual that you wear yourself out trying in vain to conquer the behavior without confronting the spirit that is behind it. This battle is not a physical war that can be won with advanced weapons and manmade knowledge. Rather, it is a spiritual battle against the rulers of darkness of this world and the spiritual wickedness that drives its ungodly and deadly behavior.

The danger in not confronting this spirit with your spiritual armament is that unless it is stopped, the spirit of Jezebel continues to spread quickly and fiercely. It's what holds entire churches captive to the controlling spirits of a handful of individuals who keep the leader and prophet of God on the run, obeying familiar spirits instead of the voice of God. The Jezebel spirit is extremely deceptive and will camouflage itself as the voice of God while setting its stage for a grand finale of destruction. People who are controlled by this spirit are often very spirited individuals who seem to always hear the voice of God. This is why you must exercise extreme caution in flocking to people who always have a "word from the Lord." You must judge all things according to the Word of God and not allow yourself to be swayed by voices that disguise themselves as the savior who's come to rescue you from your barren land. The Jezebel spirit's desire is to keep you from hearing the voice of God, and instead lead you according to her doctrine and beliefs.

I remember growing up around very dogmatic and religious individuals. They were so in tuned to the voices of those whose doctrines ruled the church that even when you showed them the truth in the Word of God they could not and would not comprehend it. Their answer always remained the same, "I know what the Bible says, but it's different from what I've been taught." Their doctrines and beliefs had more power than the Word of God that was shown to them, which revealed the truth. When man's voice becomes more dominant than the voice and power of God, this is a very dangerous predicament in which to remain. The only way to overcome this spirit is to confront it with the spirit of God. As long as Jezebel knows that she is in charge, she will continue to rule and wreak havoc.

The first step in overcoming this controlling spirit is in exercising the power of discernment. I have never seen a Jezebel spirit freely admit that it was operating in that manner without confronting it first. Oftentimes those who are under its spell will attack you for coming against what they've mistakenly seen as the spirit of God. Controlling and manipulative individuals often come off as very kind and caring persons and those who are not spiritual won't always immediately see the hidden motives of this cunning force until it slithers its way so deep into the life of a person that he or she cannot find the power from which to break free. Jezebel preys on the vulnerabilities and weaknesses of others. It was not by mistake that Jezebel married Ahab. The Jezebels of this world cleave to two types of individuals: (1) the corrupt, (2) and the naïve.

Those who are already corrupt in their actions are more susceptible to Jezebel's bewitching spirit and can assist her in carrying out her ungodly and hidden motives. Immediately upon marrying Jezebel, Ahab built an altar to worship the false god Baal. This was only the beginning of what lie ahead for the kingdom that would exist under Ahab's rule.

Naïve individuals, preoccupied with their own insecurities and failures, are bewitched by the controlling force of Jezebel's seducing spirit. They leave the decisions concerning their personal lives in her hands to do with whatever she so desires. She uses the ignorance of the naïve as a conduit to destroy leaders and other godly individuals whom she can not reach.

I've seen countless of individuals turn on trusted individuals due to the whisper of a Jezebel that was able to convince these persons that their loved ones were the enemy. In fact, the seductive whisper of this spirit has caused countless families, friends, marriages, and even churches to crumble as dust to the ground. Jezebel comes and pats you on the back, reminds you of what a good job you're doing, and how everyone else is against you except her. If you need to hear that you're a great preacher, this is what Jezebel tells you. If you need to hear that you're perfect in all things, Jezebel will accommodate this request and puff your ego just enough to incorporate her way of thinking into your mind-set and psyche. She is so subtle and smooth that you won't even realize that you're being subjected to this cunning spirit until it's too late. Some people never recover, and just as the false prophets died with her in the Bible days, so do some of those today who allow this seductive force to lead them from their places of spiritual covering and into her web of deceit.

With her much fair speech she caused him to yield, with the flattering of her lips she forced him. He goeth after her straightway, as an ox goeth to the slaughter, or as a fool to the correction of the stocks; till a dart strike through his liver; as a bird hasteth to the snare, and knoweth not that it is for his life. (Proverbs 7:21–23)

Every attack that the enemy launches against the believer is for a purpose. The spirit of deception is launched to kill, steal, and destroy destiny. Now that you've learned how to recognize it in operation, you must now break free from it if you've found yourself or others captivated by this annoying spell:

1. **Confront it.** This is not a spirit to be toyed with. You cannot skirt around the real life issues when it comes to this spirit, neither can you address it mildly in hopes that it will go away. As bold as she is to come against the children of God, we must be as equally bold in our quest to overcome this manipulative force. Call it what it is, renounce it, and get ready for a fight.

2. **Arm yourself.** When Ezekiel confronted
   Jezebel she didn't just acquiesce to his commands. Instead, she became infuriated and
   sought to annihilate him for exposing her
   limitations. Anytime you confront a controlling spirit you must also get ready to fight
   the good fight of faith, knowing that the
   weapons of your warfare are not carnal. (See
   2 Corinthians 10:4.) This is a real life spiritual battle that can only be won by remaining steadfast to the truth concerning the
   will of God and exercising the power that He
   has endowed within you to cast down every
   stronghold.

*Wherefore seeing we also are compassed about
with so great a cloud of witnesses, let us lay
aside every weight, and the sin which doth so
easily beset us.* (Hebrews 12:1)

You will never truly be successful by continuing to
hold on to things that God has instructed you to get
rid of. What weights are currently holding you captive
and keeping you from realizing your success? What outside influences have crept into your life causing you to
lose focus of the power of Jesus' death and resurrection?
Surprisingly enough, you could now be operating under
the bewitching spell of someone who has whispered just
one seemingly innocent thought into your ear, which
caused you to question the will and voice of God. There
are many things that the enemy uses to deceive us and
keep us outside of the will of God. The only sure way to
know His voice is to study His Word, commune with Him

in prayer, and learn His voice. *"My sheep hear my voice, and I know them, and they follow me"* (John 10:27).

There is an undeniable relationship between a shepherd and his sheep. When you know who your God is, you recognize His voice and flee from those that are strange. Anyone or anything promising you better results than what God can give you or what He has promised is a sure sign that the enemy is in operation. And though we often like to see speedy results concerning our wants and desires we must remember that God is both the Author and Finisher. He has a plan for our lives; He knows the outcome, how long it will take for us to get there, and the road that we must travel to reach each and every destination.

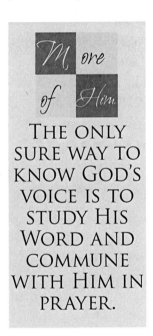

THE ONLY SURE WAY TO KNOW GOD'S VOICE IS TO STUDY HIS WORD AND COMMUNE WITH HIM IN PRAYER.

Think of how differently things might have turned out for Saul if only he'd simply followed the Lord's command. Instead, he allowed what he saw in the natural to cloud his spiritual vision, and when your spiritual vision becomes obstructed, your decision-making process begins a downward spiral. If we obey the voice of God, He promised, *"I give unto them eternal life; and they shall never perish, neither shall any man pluck them out of my hand"* (John 10:28).

Chapter Eight

THE SPIRIT'S
UNIFYING WORK

Chapter Eight

THE SPIRIT'S UNIFYING WORK

We've already talked about how the Holy Spirit serves as our Comforter, our Guide, and our Source of selfless love. But did you know He's a unifier, a mender of broken relationships? The Old Testament story of Daniel is a good place to further our study.

DANIEL'S STICKY SITUATIONS

During the reign of Judah's King Jehoiakim, King Nebuchadnezzar of Babylon besieged Jerusalem. (See Daniel 1:1.) In overthrowing the government, he took the Israelites into captivity and carried them into the borders of Babylon. The king separated from the group those young men who were intelligent, wise, and without blemish, those considered most valuable and worthy of standing in the king's palace. (See Daniel 1:3–4.)

Included in this group were Shadrach, Meshach, Abednego, and Daniel.

EVEN THOUGH DANIEL FOUND HIMSELF IN CAPTIVITY, HE REALLY WAS AS FREE AS CAN BE.

Even though Daniel found himself in captivity, he really was as free as can be. You see, when the Holy Spirit becomes your Guide, when you allow the Lord to direct your paths, captivity is only as bad as you allow it to be.

Maybe your bondage isn't physical, as Daniel's was. Maybe you're not behind bars or stuck in physical confinement but trapped instead by an oppressed mind, weaknesses, and failures. Nonetheless, you *can* maintain the victory that the Lord has given and draw from Him the strength that you need for difficult times. God's Word promises,

My grace is sufficient for thee: for my strength is made perfect in weakness. Most gladly therefore will I rather glory in my infirmities, that the power of Christ may rest upon me. (2 Corinthians 12:9)

The Comforter is our gift from God. *"Not by might, nor by power, but by my spirit, saith the LORD of hosts"* (Zechariah 4:6).

Further in the book of Daniel we find that this man of God rose to a place of prominence, becoming ruler over the province of Babylon. What a leap for someone who was supposed to be a prisoner! But while the king respected Daniel's opinion, credibility, and devotion, others resented his favor with the king and conspired to ruin Daniel's credibility. When they found Daniel blameless, they conspired to attack the one thing that Daniel held most dear—his relationship with his God. (See Daniel 6:1–8.)

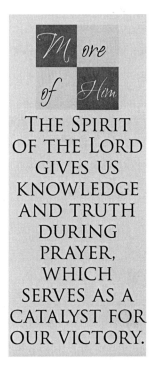

More of Him

THE SPIRIT OF THE LORD GIVES US KNOWLEDGE AND TRUTH DURING PRAYER, WHICH SERVES AS A CATALYST FOR OUR VICTORY.

An application in this story for today is this: When the enemy finds you blameless, his next attempt is to hinder your communication with God. The devil knows that the Spirit of the Lord gives us knowledge and truth during prayer, which serves as a catalyst for our deliverance and victory; Satan wants to prevent us from receiving God's truth and knowledge. That's why he tries to impede our communication with God, just as he did with Daniel:

> *Then these presidents and princes assembled together to the king, and said thus unto him, King Darius, live for ever. All the presidents of the kingdom, the governors, and the princes, the counsellors, and the captains, have consulted together to establish a royal statute, and to make a firm decree, that whosoever shall ask a petition of any God or man for thirty days, save of thee, O king, he shall be cast into the den of lions.*
>
> (Daniel 6:6–7)

Because Daniel had the boldness of the Holy Spirit on his side and a solid relationship with the Lord, he was not deterred by this obvious attack. Instead he continued to pray as usual, three times a day with the windows open. Daniel was not afraid, nor would he submit to worshipping or praying to anything or anyone other than the true and living God. (See verse 10.) When the Holy Spirit is present, people do not shy away from issues; instead, they confront their situations with boldness and stand firm in what they believe.

THE HOLY SPIRIT IS INDEED A COMFORTER. WE CAN COUNT ON HIM TO SEE US THROUGH EVERY TRIAL.

Once he was found praying, Daniel was thrown into the den of lions. Because of the favor of the Lord upon Daniel's life, however, Daniel prevailed and the mouths of the lions were shut (Daniel 6:22). Daniel, because of his prayer life, was in direct contact with the Father and was accustomed to the Lord's answering His prayers. The Holy Spirit is indeed a Comforter; so even when our flesh resists and becomes anxious, we can count on Him to see us through every trial. Even when we are overwhelmed by life's situations and don't know how we should pray, the Holy Spirit intercedes for us. God's Word encourages us with this truth:

Likewise the Spirit also helpeth our infirmities: for we know not what we should pray for as we ought: but the Spirit itself maketh intercession for us with groanings which cannot be uttered.

(Romans 8:26)

The Greek word for *groan* simply means "articulation." The Spirit articulates our needs to the Father.

The Spirit may speak languages such as Spanish, Greek, Chinese, or German, or the language of heaven. *"For if I pray in an unknown tongue, my spirit prayeth, but my understanding is unfruitful"* (1 Corinthians 14:14). You many not understand all that you're saying while speaking in tongues, but you know that God understands and He knows exactly what you need.

AN AWAKENING DREAM: INSIGHT INTO DANIEL 10

I had never paid much attention to Daniel 10 until my seven-day dream, which specifically dealt with this Scripture passage and its meaning. In the dream I saw the entire world praying. I knew it was the entire world because I could see both night and day at once, and everyone was praying. As they were praying in cars, convalescent homes, open fields, shopping malls, and houses, a mist came out of their mouths; it floated up through ceilings and through roofs.

Then, as if suddenly snatched from this scene, I found myself traveling through the principalities of Satan. I saw a man sitting on a throne with his hands resting over the arms of the chair. He had the most beautifully manicured nails. He was dressed in a white suit and had silky gray hair, which was neatly slicked back above his brow.

I knew this man was Satan, even though His appearance was completely contrary to every image I'd ever had of Him. And that is one of the reasons the enemy of our souls is such a great deceiver; he doesn't wear a red suit, carry a pitchfork, or have horns and a long tail. He takes on a form that entices and draws others to him so that he can capture them in his web of deceit.

In my dream a great wall extended around the entire world. It was as if Satan had enclosed the whole world within a hedge. In every nook and cranny of the wall stood demons. As they looked at the wall, with pen and pads in hand, they recorded the prayers of the saints. Suddenly, I woke up, but the dream was still very vivid and lingered in my mind.

I later fell asleep again, only to return to the same dream. As the saints prayed, their prayers were plastered against the wall. The demons, which were disfigured animal-like creatures, wrote down the prayers of the saints. Suddenly I saw an angel come down out of the principalities. As the angel appeared, all the demons simultaneously wrestled him to the floor and pulled out of his hand what he had been holding. In the dream my body shook because God was showing me the reason that many of us don't get what God promises: We give up too easily. Every prayer that you pray is heard in Satan's kingdom, unless it is prayed in tongues. After the demons had wrestled the angel to the floor, I woke up. The Lord took me to Daniel 10.

When I heard the voice of his words, then was I in a deep sleep on my face, and my face toward the ground. And, behold, an hand touched me, which set me upon my knees and upon the palms of my hands. And he said unto me, O Daniel, a man greatly beloved, understand the words that I speak unto thee, and stand upright: for unto thee am I now sent. And when he had spoken this word unto me, I stood trembling. Then said he unto me, Fear not, Daniel: for from the first day that thou didst set thine heart to understand, and to chasten thyself before thy God, thy words were heard, and I am come for thy words. But the prince of the kingdom of Persia withstood me one and twenty days: but, lo, Michael, one of the chief princes, came to help me; and I remained there with the kings of Persia. Now I am come to make thee understand what shall befall thy people in the latter days: for yet the vision is for many days. (Daniel 10:9–14)

It's clear, then, and important for us to understand, that we are fighting against supernatural forces that we cannot see. Many times our ministries are hindered because we allow spirits to wrestle God's angel down and rip from his hand the thing that God desires for us to have.

Finally God said, "Enough is enough. Every time I try to get a word to My people, they can't get it because Satan, the power of the air, hinders them from receiving the gifts I have to give. I'm going to change some things."

So now, when the saints begin to pray, the walls in the principalities are covered with words spoken in tongues that have not been interpreted. Satan and his demonic hosts try, to no avail, to decode what is going on and to intercept the petitions of God's people. What they discover, though, is that they can't decipher the prayers on the wall.

The saints of old used to sing a song, *"Oh, the blood of Jesus! It will never lose its power!"* God does have all power, and His Son's blood is covering your prayers. Every time Satan tries to reach you and snatch you away from God's covering, he's forced to flee; he simply cannot deal with the blood of Christ.

GOD DOES HAVE ALL THE POWER, AND HIS SON'S BLOOD IS COVERING YOUR PRAYERS.

In this way, the Holy Spirit is a unifier, a mender of the communication between God and His children. The work that Jesus began—to bring us back into communion with the Father—the Holy Spirit continues; He intercedes for us, presenting our requests to God in groanings that speak to God more completely and perfectly than our human tongues ever could.

A DIVIDED PEOPLE

This story of Daniel provides the background for another unifying work of the Spirit: the reuniting of God's people with each other. You see, the people of

Israel were divided, separated, scattered, and shattered during Daniel's time.

> *In the third year of the reign of Jehoiakim king of Judah came Nebuchadnezzar king of Babylon unto Jerusalem, and besieged it. And the Lord gave Jehoiakim king of Judah into his hand, with part of the vessels of the house of God: which he carried into the land of Shinar to the house of his god; and he brought the vessels into the treasure house of his god.* (Daniel 1:1–2)

Without going into a lengthy study of Daniel 1, we can note that it contains a brief historical account of how several of the tribes of Judah were dispersed throughout the existing nations of the earth. Psalm 137:1–4 captures the emotions of Israel at that time:

> *By the rivers of Babylon, there we sat down, yea, we wept, when we remembered Zion. We hanged our harps upon the willows in the midst thereof. For there they that carried us away captive required of us a song; and they that wasted us required of us mirth, saying, Sing us one of the songs of Zion. How shall we sing the Lord's song in a strange land?*

THE HOPE FOR DRY BONES

The good news is, God did not leave Israel a shattered and scattered nation. He promised to bring it together again, to unite its people once more. One of the earliest and most vivid prophecies of this reuniting work is found in Ezekiel. There, the Lord led Ezekiel to a graveyard filled with bones, and miraculously He brought the bones together to form a body. As God brought these dead and separated graveyard bones together into new living forms, so too did He promise to restore Israel back to life. Let's take a look at Ezekiel 37:

> *The hand of the LORD was upon me, and carried me out in the spirit of the LORD, and set me down in the midst of the valley which was full of bones, and caused me to pass by them round about: and, behold, there were very many in the open valley; and, lo, they were very dry. And he said unto me, Son of man, can these bones live? And I answered, O Lord GOD, thou knowest. Again he said unto me, Prophesy upon these bones, and say unto them, O ye dry bones, hear the word of the LORD. Thus saith the Lord GOD unto these bones; Behold, I will cause breath to enter into you, and ye shall live: and I will lay sinews upon you, and will bring up flesh upon you, and cover you with skin, and put breath in you, and ye shall live; and ye shall know that I am the LORD. So I prophesied as I was commanded: and as I prophesied, there was a noise, and behold a shaking, and the bones came together, bone to his bone. And when I beheld, lo, the sinews and the flesh came up upon them, and the skin covered them above: but there was no breath in them. Then said he unto me, Prophesy unto the wind, prophesy, son of man, and say to the wind, Thus saith the Lord GOD; Come from the four winds, O breath, and breathe upon these slain, that they may live. So I prophesied as he commanded me, and the breath came into them,*

and they lived, and stood up upon their feet, an exceeding great army. Then he said unto me, Son of man, these bones are the whole house of Israel: behold, they say, Our bones are dried, and our hope is lost: we are cut off for our parts. Therefore prophesy and say unto them, Thus saith the Lord GOD; Behold, O my people, I will open your graves, and cause you to come up out of your graves, and bring you into the land of Israel. And ye shall know that I am the LORD, when I have opened your graves, O my people, and brought you up out of your graves, and shall put my spirit in you, and ye shall live, and I shall place you in your own land: then shall ye know that I the LORD have spoken it, and performed it, saith the LORD.
(Ezekiel 37:1–14)

Ezekiel 37:1 deals with traveling or entering into the vision of God. The next verse refers to the gathering of information. And the following verse is a challenge: *"Son of man, can these bones live?"* Ezekiel answered, *"O Lord GOD, thou knowest."* In other words, he was saying, "I am submitting myself to Your will. Whatever You say, I will do." In Ezekiel 37:4, God told Ezekiel to prophesy, which means "to proclaim," "to pre-announce," or "to preach." Ezekiel was admonished by the Lord to prophesy unto these bones, to decree to them, *"Hear the word of the LORD."*

Ezekiel was then carried into the great valley, through the collection of bones. Remember, *"the valley"* refers to a graveyard, and the graveyard in this particular text represents the nations in which Israel's people were trapped. The people of Israel were trapped in these nations for hundreds of years. Ezekiel was prophesying to a nation that was *"cut off for* [its] *parts"* (v. 11). Eventually the people of Israel would end up in Medes, Persia, Mesopotamia, Cyrene, and other nations. Ezekiel, however, brought a word of hope from God. The people of Israel had lost their identity, their hope, their ability to worship. Ezekiel reminded them of their history and of the promising future that lay ahead: the complete reunification of God's people with Himself and with each other.

THE FULFILLMENT: PENTECOST

The fulfillment of Ezekiel's symbolic prophecy happened many years later, on the Day of Pentecost:

And there were dwelling at Jerusalem Jews, devout men, out of every nation under heaven. Now when this was noised abroad, the multitude came together, and were confounded, because that every man heard them speak in his own language. And they were all amazed and marvelled, saying one to another, Behold, are not all these which speak Galilaeans? And how hear we every man in our own tongue, wherein we were born? Parthians, and Medes, and Elamites, and the dwellers in Mesopotamia, and in Judaea, and Cappadocia, in Pontus, and Asia, Phrygia, and Pamphylia, in Egypt, and in the parts of Libya about Cyrene, and strangers of Rome, Jews and proselytes, Cretes and Arabians, we do hear them speak in our tongues the wonderful works of God.

And they were all amazed, and were in doubt, saying one to another, What meaneth this?

(Acts 2:5–12)

Notice especially verse five: *"And there were dwelling at Jerusalem Jews, devout men, out of every nation under heaven."* The statement *"out of every nation under heaven"* is easy to understand. America did not exist at that time, neither did many other nations, states, and provinces that exist today. When the Word of God says, *"every nation under heaven,"* it's talking about the existing nations at that particular time, at the time of Pentecost. A list of some of those nations are given in verses nine and ten:

Parthians, and Medes, and Elamites, and the dwellers in Mesopotamia, and in Judaea, and Cappadocia, in Pontus, and Asia, Phrygia, and Pamphylia, in Egypt, and in the parts of Libya about Cyrene, and strangers of Rome, Jews and proselytes, Cretes and Arabians.

The Jewish people were living in all those nations. The Jews who had been scattered during Daniel's time, the Jews who had received Ezekiel's message of hope years before—the ancestors of these scattered people now gathered together for the initial indwelling of the Holy Spirit. In Acts 2 is the fulfillment of Ezekiel 38. The Holy Spirit once more did a great unifying work.

FROM BABEL TO PENTECOST

The Tower of Babel can help us understand the unifying work of the Holy Spirit. Before we can gain this insight, however, we need to review what happens when men try to usurp God's authority.

> *And the whole earth was of one language, and of one speech. And it came to pass, as they journeyed from the east, that they found a plain in the land of Shinar; and they dwelt there. And they said one to another, Go to, let us make brick, and burn them thoroughly. And they had brick for stone, and slime had they for mortar. And they said, Go to, let us build us a city and a tower, whose top may reach unto heaven; and let us make us a name, lest we be scattered abroad upon the face of the whole earth. And the LORD came down to see the city and the tower, which the children of men builded. And the LORD said, Behold, the people is one, and they have all one language; and this they begin to do: and now nothing will be restrained from them, which they have imagined to do. Go to, let us go down, and there confound their language, that they may not understand one another's speech. So the LORD scattered them abroad from thence upon the face of all the earth: and they left off to build the city. Therefore is the name of it called Babel; because the LORD did there confound the language of all the earth: and from thence did the LORD scatter them abroad upon the face of all the earth.*
>
> (Genesis 11:1–9)

At Babel, a king by the name of Nimrod was building a wonderful and glorious monument to himself, the type of monument that was built during ancient times.

This reflected Nimrod's pride as well as the pride of the people; they thought they were going to build a tower up to the heavens. This really isn't too much different from the ambitions of many people today. The only difference between Nimrod's times and ours is that men no longer build the structured towers of Babel or ancient pyramids. We call them something different now: skyscrapers.

From the start of time, men have tried to reach the heavens relying only on human ingenuity. In our modern day, the race to reach the heavens thrives in corporate America. From the CNN Towers of Toronto, Canada, to the Empire State Building of New York City, and the Sears Tower of Chicago, Illinois, man, in his quest to reach the heavens for power, wisdom, and knowledge, has not detoured from ancient mystical beliefs that the sky can be reached. In corporate America, the floor you are on suggests the level of your success and power. A corner office on the top floor of a tall building with windows overlooking the city implies that you have really reached the heavens.

So this young man, Nimrod, was approached by his astrologers and chief priests to build a temple that would allow them to reach into the heavens. As they called in their architects and designers, the ideal architectural plan was finally completed. By one historian's account of archeological findings, the tower of Babel was built thousands of feet into the sky. One of the things you can't deny is that, during this time when there were no cranes or modern technology of any sort, these men completed quite a feat. They came to a place of oneness where anything that they could imagine was possible.

Much to the amazement of everyone, although this structure was already so high, they decided to build it a little higher. They also began constructing a dome, a place for the priests and astrologers to conduct their work by studying the heavens and the stars. And God became angry. God became angry because the inhabitants of the earth decided to try to enter heaven without coming through the doorway of righteousness. They used what they thought would be a mighty power force—they used unity. When a body is unified, it can do almost anything.

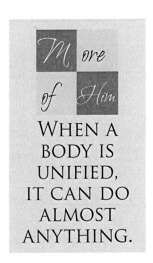

WHEN A BODY IS UNIFIED, IT CAN DO ALMOST ANYTHING.

The Scriptures say that they were of one mind, one heart, and that they could do anything they imagined.

*And the L*ORD *said, Behold, the people is one, and they have all one language; and this they begin to do: and now nothing will be restrained from them, which they have imagined to do.*

(Genesis 11:6)

It is here that God released a spirit of confusion, which is how the tower got its name. In a split second, men began to speak other languages that sounded like babble to each other.

*Go to, let us go down, and there confound their language, that they may not understand one another's speech. So the L*ORD *scattered them* *abroad from thence upon the face of all the earth: and they left off to build the city. Therefore is the name of it called Babel; because the LORD did there confound the language of all the earth: and from thence did the LORD scatter them abroad upon the face of all the earth.* (Genesis 11:7–9)

After chattering from one person to the other, they began to find partners whom they could understand. The Scripture says that they began to form regencies and camps, then countries and nations.

Now one may ask, "What is the relationship between Babel and Pentecost?" The answer is simple. In Genesis 11, God used tongues to divide the nations. But in Acts 2, He used tongues to bring the nations back together. The hope that was lost at Babel was reclaimed at Pentecost. So Pentecost not only releases the church; it also brings into focus God's long-term plan to bring us back to our first love.

And when the day of Pentecost was fully come, they were all with one accord in one place. And suddenly there came a sound from heaven as of a rushing mighty wind, and it filled all the house where they were sitting. And there appeared unto them cloven tongues like as of fire, and it sat upon each of them. (Acts 2:1–3)

Chapter Nine

EMPOWERED BY HIS GRACE

Chapter Nine

EMPOWERED BY HIS GRACE

any myths have surfaced regarding the cognizance of the dead; where they are and what they're doing. Though there are varying opinions regarding the matter, one thing remains sure...those who are dead are no longer engaged in the affairs of the world. This same scenario holds true with those who are dead to sin.

Romans 6:1 says, *"What shall we say then? Shall we continue in sin, that grace may abound?"* We often hear this Scripture quoted but rarely do those who hear it actually understand the significance of the points that Paul was attempting to convey. We often translate the verses to mean "God's sustaining power in sin" when in fact, grace is extended to those who have died to sin, which verses two through four go on to further prove. *"God forbid. How shall we, that are dead to sin, live any longer therein? Know ye not, that so many of us as were baptized into his death?"* In other words, where sin is, much more grace abounds. Those who are "dead" to sin and crucified with Christ are no longer slaves to sin. Through the grace of God, you are now dead to sin, which means that your decisions in life are no longer dominated and ruled by the sinful nature. The grace of God is liberating. It frees us from ourselves and allows the presence of God to become the ruling force behind our way of thinking, giving us spiritual insight into the unknown, which allows us to flourish beyond the comprehension of mankind's finite understanding. His grace frees us from sin and we are no longer slaves to the old man, but are able to walk in the newness of life, and the liberty of Christ wherein He has made us free.

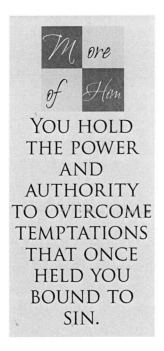

YOU HOLD THE POWER AND AUTHORITY TO OVERCOME TEMPTATIONS THAT ONCE HELD YOU BOUND TO SIN.

Knowing this, that our old man is crucified with him, that the body of sin might be destroyed, that henceforth we should not serve sin. For he that is dead is freed from sin. (Romans 6:6–7)

As an individual who is dead to sin, you hold the power and authority to overcome temptations that once held you bound to sin. As children operating under the sinful nature, we often take on the attitude: "The devil made me do it." But as we begin to turn from the milk and digest the meat of the word we begin to realize that the devil no longer has the authority to "make" us engage in sinful acts to appease the flesh. We often wonder why it seems that we struggle more to overcome bad habits after salvation than we did before submitting our lives to the Lord. The truth of the matter is that it's not always that we're struggling more, but once we're saved, we're more cognizant of the fact that we've lived so long with the same problems that it feels foreign for us to finally break free from what's held us bound. The children of Israel voiced this same complaint as they wandered about in the wilderness. They rebuked Moses for freeing them from bondage. The devil knows that he no longer has control over your life so he attempts to intensify the temptations of the past so that you're more inclined to acquiesce to his deceitful mirage of satisfaction. Much like the alcoholic who desires to revert to drinking when the pressures of life become too much to bear, the same often holds true when the believer's life becomes more focused on the tests and trials than God's power to deliver him from them all.

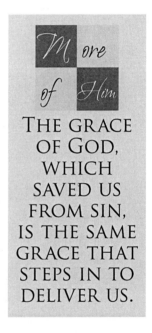

More of Him

THE GRACE OF GOD, WHICH SAVED US FROM SIN, IS THE SAME GRACE THAT STEPS IN TO DELIVER US.

Due to human nature, our first inclination in the midst of adversity is to find the swiftest route of relief, and all too often the enemy is waiting patiently to offer us a way of escape from our seemingly unbearable pain. Thankfully, however, the grace of God, which saved us from sin, is the same grace that steps in to deliver us from the snare of the enemy's trap. Because we are no longer slaves to sin, we recognize that the best way to maintain our newfound freedom is to rely on the sustaining power of God through prayer. When the old man has died, reverting to the sinful nature is no longer an option. Instead, remain steadfast and unmovable, always abounding in the work of the Lord. It's no longer your flesh that you're relying upon to keep you from sin because the old man has been crucified. Now it is the Spirit who dwells within you who gives you the power to overcome the sins of the world.

> *And if Christ be in you, the body is dead because of sin; but the Spirit is life because of righteousness.* (Romans 8:10)

The trick of the enemy is to make you feel powerless when, if fact, if you've died to the flesh and been resurrected with Christ, you've been cured from the sinful nature. You now hold the power to overcome whatever is attempting to overcome you.

> *Who his own self bare our sins in his own body on the tree, that we, being dead to sins, should live unto righteousness: by whose stripes ye were healed.* (1 Peter 2:24)

Here, the purpose of Christ's death is made plain to see: *"that we, being dead to sins, should live unto righteousness."* In order for righteousness to rule and reign, we must first die to sin. Many of our struggles with this originate from our erroneous way of thinking. While we're quick to seek God's forgiveness of sins, we mistakenly fail to recognize the absolute necessity of making an inward change. This is also why the same individuals can be seen at the altars week after week seeking forgiveness for the same thing that He forgave them of the week before. Though they continue to ask God to forgive them, they leave the church and go back to their same environments, rely on their same way of thinking, and make little or no effort to kill the root cause of the problem. God doesn't just want to forgive you of your sins, He wants you to benefit from His many blessings that He left as an inheritance to those who submit to His will. Hosea 4:6 says, *"My people are destroyed for lack of knowledge."* Without knowing the truth concerning the Word of God, you don't recognize the fact that you've been endowed with power from on high to overcome the world. You feel that you're too weak to fight, too powerless to resist.

This is where faith and knowledge must coincide. You must develop knowledge concerning the truth of the Word of God and exercise faith in knowing that what the Word of God says is true. The more you study and spend time with God, the less susceptible you become to the tricks and snares of the enemy.

In the natural there is a death and burial. In the spirit, however, there is a death, a burial, and a resurrection. When you give your life to the Lord, the carnal man dies. Then there is a baptismal process. During water baptism you are immersed into the water, which represents the burial of the old man, but when you're lifted out of the water, it signifies your resurrection into the newness of life. It's not the actual baptism that saves you, but it's through your confession to God and repentance that you are received into the kingdom. Water baptism is an outward show of an inward work that has already been done. Galatians 3:25–28 reminds us that faith in God makes us His children. We are no longer separated by human boundaries, but we become one in Christ. Being water baptized is not just a religious ritual with no pertinent results. It's an act of faith in God. Therefore, you should never approach water baptism as an insignificant ceremony, but rather a spiritual appointment with destiny that has the capacity to greatly change your life. If you could see in the spirit, you'd see the old man being put off as you become one with the Spirit of Christ.

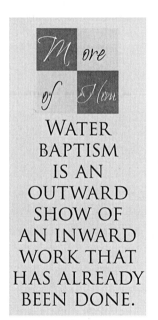

WATER BAPTISM IS AN OUTWARD SHOW OF AN INWARD WORK THAT HAS ALREADY BEEN DONE.

The grave and the dead things that once plagued your life no longer have power over you. The mistake that we often make is in our futile attempts to conquer the grave of our own will instead of recognizing the Holy Spirit who gives us the power to overcome all things. Regardless of how many times you are prayed for, if you don't believe in or are unaware of the significance of the Spirit's power that dwells within you, you will continue to fall for the same traps and snares. This is not to say that you will no longer have moments of temptation after the Spirit of God comes into your life, but that those notions to sin will no longer control you as they did before submitting your life to the Lord.

For years I struggled with addictions and bad habits that hindered my walk with God. It wasn't until I came into the full knowledge of His power that I was able to walk in liberty. Perhaps you've struggled endlessly with the same problems year after year. It often seems hopeless and that there is no relief possibly in sight. One touch from God, however, can heal a multiplicity of faults. The devil deceives us into thinking that prayer is useless and that nothing can alleviate the pain. He sends us on wild goose chases seeking deliverance and relief when the answer to what we need already resides within us. If we could simply hold fast to this truth and not give up, even when it seems that there is no hope, then we'd experience victory over many more wars instead of constantly losing battles that have already been won on our behalf.

When I think of all the lives that God has touched and changed through the messages that I've preached, I think to myself, "What if I'd given up, thrown in the towel, or given in to death?" Had I given up, I would never have been able to experience the pleasure of a mother being delivered from drugs, a life saved who was about to commit suicide, the relief of a man being set free from demonic possession, or witness the pressures of a young boy and girl being lifted after experiencing years of abuse and finally being able to enjoy a childhood of safety. Think of the countless numbers of people who are waiting for you so that they might be set free. You could hold the keys to their deliverance through your testimony. Share with them the truth concerning God's grace, His sustaining power during difficult times, and His obsession in seeing you set free.

It is through our circumstances that God teaches us how to be a blessing to others. Your trials and tribulations are not designed for your defeat. Rather, they are allowed as a place of higher learning. When you graduate, you feel equipped with knowledge and power and go on to use those experiences to teach others.

Romans 8:28 says, *"And we know that all things work together for good to them that love God, to them who are the called according to his purpose."* Notice that it says, *"according to his purpose."* Once you give your life to the Lord, you are called according to God's purpose and not your own. This means that regardless of what you go through as a believer, God is to be glorified. What you set out to accomplish in your own will might fall as dust to ground, but when we do God's will He will be glorified. God doesn't know failure and He has no room for defeat. So when defeat in your life looks inevitable, remain steadfast in what you know as the truth of God and realize that He is simply making room for His glory to be magnified.

> *My brethren, count it all joy when ye fall into divers temptations. Knowing this, that the trying of your faith worketh patience. But let patience have her perfect work, that ye may be perfect and entire, wanting nothing.* (James 1:2–4)

Even when you fall into *"divers temptations"* God has a plan and purpose for your life, so count it all joy. When your faith is tried, you really begin to learn who God is and the limitless possibilities of His goodness and grace. After submitting your life to Him, anything that is not like Him will eventually be purged out. Because He is obsessed with fulfilling His Word concerning you and because you've become one with Him, there is only room for His Word within you to reside.

Growing up I often heard the saints erroneously teach that once you receive the Holy Spirit, all of your troubles and trials are over. Quite the contrary, James chapter one reminds us that you might fall into *"divers temptations,"* but count it all joy. It's what you do during these trying times that makes all the difference. The Holy Spirit is not some ogre who ties your hands behind your back and forces you to behave according to His will. Rather, we are neither bond nor free, which means that we are no longer slaves to sin, but free to walk in the liberty wherein Christ has made us free.

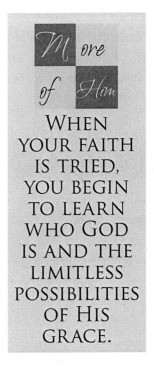

WHEN YOUR FAITH IS TRIED, YOU BEGIN TO LEARN WHO GOD IS AND THE LIMITLESS POSSIBILITIES OF HIS GRACE.

It's this freedom in Christ that quickens us just when we're about to give up or attempt to do things our way. Because He is a part of us, we can go nowhere without Him and do nothing without Him being a part of what we do. It's His presence that we feel when we're about to sin or about to throw in the towel. He ever so gently speaks to us, taps us on the shoulder, and reminds us to remain in the will of the Lord. Whether we choose to listen or disobey will ultimately determine the outcome of our situation.

It's said that it is darkest right before the brink of day. Many times, right when you're right at the brink of your breakthrough is when the enemy sends a smoke-screen to cloud the victory that's waiting for you on the other side of the unbearable nightmare in which you've been living. Today more than ever we're living in a day of mass deception. Just as Jesus warned of mass deception regarding those who'd come to deceive many into believing that they are Christ (Matthew 24), so it is with the enemy in his cunning moves to belittle the power of Christ that's alive and effective in your life. With the Holy Spirit as your guide, you become less susceptible to the cunning tactics of Satan that come to revert your attention away from the victory that God has promised.

The devil presents you with many options to provide you a way of escape but the Spirit of God always reminds you that God's way is perfect and that He alone holds the means to meet your every need. People often ask how to tell if their actions are within the will of God or a trap to dig them deeper into a point of no return. There are several ways to distinguish the will of God from the deceitful enticements of the devil when it comes to seeking a peaceful resolution to what's currently plaguing your life. If you can answer "yes" to any of the following questions, it's more likely than not that deception, and not God, is the one attempting to steer your reaction to a vulnerable situation:

1. Does the solution require you to commit sin?

2. Is the solution to the problem causing you more stress than the problem itself?

The grace of God and the Holy Spirit in the believer's life is so prevalent that even in the midst of your ordeal,

God covers you and protects you from the fall. *"God is faithful, who will not suffer you to be tempted above that ye are able; but will with the temptation also make a way to escape, that ye may be able to bear it."* If the way of escape that is being presented to you causes you to become entrapped in another area of bondage, you can rest assured that you're not in the will of God. When in doubt remember the promise of 2 Corinthians 12:9, *"My grace is sufficient for thee: for my strength is made perfect in weakness."* In your weakest moments is when the grace of God and His strength is being glorified.

Chapter Ten

FROM DEATH TO LIFE—
RAISED TO SERVE

Chapter Ten

FROM DEATH TO LIFE— RAISED TO SERVE

The breath of God's Spirit has always been the source of His life-producing plan. The Old Testament prophet Ezekiel learned this through God's amazing prophetic picture: Just as the lifeless skeletal bones formed a body, dead and defeated Israel would come to life.

Thus saith the Lord God unto these bones; Behold, I will cause breath to enter into you, and ye shall live: and I will lay sinews upon you, and will bring up flesh upon you, and cover you with skin, and put breath in you, and ye shall live; and ye shall know that I am the Lord. So I prophesied as I was commanded: and as I prophesied, there was a noise, and behold a shaking, and the bones came together, bone to his bone. (Ezekiel 37:5–7)

God's Spirit brought life when Jesus breathed the breath of life into the disciples. These were the first human beings to receive God's re-creative life as born-again men.

Then said Jesus to them again, Peace be unto you: as my Father hath sent me, even so send I you. And when he had said this, he breathed on them, and saith unto them, Receive ye the Holy Ghost. (John 20:21–22)

God's breath brought new life at the Day of Pentecost too. The disciples who stayed in Jerusalem were visited by a mighty rushing wind.

And suddenly there came a sound from heaven as of a rushing mighty wind, and it filled all the house where they were sitting. (Acts 2:2)

ONCE GOD SAVES AND FILLS US, HE WANTS TO USE US.

God always has a purpose in breathing new life into His children. Once He saves us and fills us, He wants to use us. Those who were faithful and stayed in Jerusalem for Pentecost were never the same again; as the book of Acts later tells us, they turned the world upside down. (See Acts 17:6.) God desires to do the same through each of His children. Let's prepare ourselves to receive His life-giving, life-restoring, life-changing breath.

WHEN WE HEAR GOD'S WORD, WE MUST CONFESS

If thou shalt confess with thy mouth the Lord Jesus, and shalt believe in thine heart that God

FROM DEATH TO LIFE—*Raised to Serve*

*hath raised him from the dead, thou shalt be
saved.* (Romans 10:9)

As we've seen through scriptural accounts of God's
life-giving Spirit, people without the energizing breath
of the Holy Spirit are mere shadows of what they can
be. God's life-changing anointing, though, falls only
upon His truth. His anointing, His Spirit, His life, will
not come to the one who is ignorant of His ways. If we
hope to receive His life-giving breath, our lives must be
steeped in Scripture, God's means for imparting truth. It
is the Word that brings the truth and ultimately makes
us free. (See John 8:32.) As Jesus said in John 6:63, *"It
is the spirit that quickeneth; the flesh profiteth nothing:
the words that I speak unto you, they are spirit, and they
are life."* Every time we hear the Word of the Lord, our
spirits are being quickened, or made alive.

Not only must we immerse our own minds and spirits in God's Word; we also need to share His truth with
others around us!

*And how shall they preach, except they be sent?
as it is written, How beautiful are the feet of them
that preach the gospel of peace, and bring glad
tidings of good things!* (Romans 10:15)

As Ezekiel was commanded to, *"Prophesy upon these
bones, and say unto them, O ye dry bones, hear the word
of the LORD"* (Ezekiel 37:4), we too must proclaim the Word
of the Lord. Remember, God set Ezekiel in the midst
of a graveyard, in the midst of skeletons desperately in
need of new life. And remember too that God provided
Ezekiel with the words to say, with the message of hope

181

that would bring life. As you obey God and listen for His leading in your life, He will set you among breathless bones craving life. And He will provide you with the wisdom to share His life-giving Word.

GOD IS BUILDING AN ARMY

So I prophesied as he commanded me, and the breath came into them, and they lived, and stood up upon their feet, an exceeding great army. (Ezekiel 37:10)

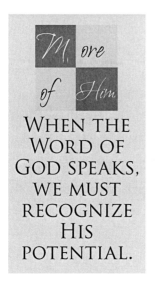

WHEN THE WORD OF GOD SPEAKS, WE MUST RECOGNIZE HIS POTENTIAL.

Another thing Ezekiel showed us is that when the Word of God speaks, we must recognize His potential. Just as God raised those dry bones and assembled them into a great army, God wants to clean us up and arm us for the great spiritual battle we're facing.

Finally, my brethren, be strong in the Lord, and in the power of his might. Put on the whole armour of God, that ye may be able to stand against the wiles of the devil. For we wrestle not against flesh and blood, but against principalities, against powers, against the rulers of the darkness of this world, against spiritual wickedness in high places. Wherefore take unto you the whole armour of God, that ye may be able to withstand in the evil day, and having done all, to stand. Stand therefore, having your loins

girt about with truth, and having on the breastplate of righteousness; and your feet shod with the preparation of the gospel of peace; above all, taking the shield of faith, wherewith ye shall be able to quench all the fiery darts of the wicked. And take the helmet of salvation, and the sword of the Spirit, which is the word of God.
(Ephesians 6:10–17)

When you hear the truth about your own situation, the best thing you can do is accept it and be obedient to the Lord's holy call, even if He leads you into a frightening situation, like facing the enemies' fiery darts. You must believe the Word of the Lord, which says, *"[I] shall put my spirit in you, and ye shall live"* (Ezekiel 37:14). For, *"I can do all things through Christ which strengtheneth me"* (Philippians 4:13).

More of Him

THE BEST THING YOU CAN DO IS ACCEPT THE LORD'S HOLY CALL, EVEN IF HE LEADS YOU INTO A FRIGHTENING SITUATION.

When the Lord told His disciples that they would receive power after the Holy Ghost came upon them, this gave them hope that they would be able to accomplish what the Lord had called them to do.

And, behold, I send the promise of my Father upon you: but tarry ye in the city of Jerusalem, until ye be endued with power from on high. And he led

them out as far as to Bethany, and he lifted up his
hands, and blessed them. And it came to pass,
while he blessed them, he was parted from them,
and carried up into heaven. And they worshipped
him, and returned to Jerusalem with great joy:
and were continually in the temple, praising and
blessing God. Amen. (Luke 24:49–53)

Before they heard of their potential, they didn't really
know how they would be able to be witnesses for Christ.
The promise of God's power, though, and His assurance
of their potential in Him made the difference.

So once you hear and read in the Word of God about
your potential, about your glorious destiny in life, it's
time to stand up to be trained as a soldier. You can be
as confident as the disciples in knowing He'll lead you to
be everything He said you can be.

And I will lay sinews upon you, and will bring
up flesh upon you, and cover you with skin, and
put breath in you, and ye shall live; and ye shall
know that I am the LORD. (Ezekiel 37:6)

You can rest in knowing that God will restore you
and lead you through life's stages. You must be will-
ing, though, to grow through those stages. Hearing the
Word of God will bring the Holy Spirit into your life.
But merely hearing the Word makes no one complete.
If we want to grow and mature to become all that we
can be, an obedient response is necessary. *"For as the*
body without the spirit is dead, so faith without works is
dead also" (James 2:26). In order to become complete,
we must first take steps in the Christian life.

FROM DEATH TO LIFE—*Raised to Serve*

*But we all, with open face beholding as in a glass
the glory of the Lord, are changed into the same
image from glory to glory, even as by the Spirit of
the Lord.* (2 Corinthians 3:18)

The story of Ezekiel's prophecy provides an image
of this step-by-step process. The first step in Ezekiel's
prophecy showed breath assembling dead, dry bones.
Next came the sinews. And then came the flesh. Hearing
and obeying are both parts of a step-by-step, orderly process, just as the assembling of the bones was a step-by-
step operation. There's more to the process of becoming a
powerful soldier than being born again. If receiving God's
gift was all it took to walk victoriously in this life, simply
sitting in church or hanging around the barracks while
others trained would be good enough. But it's not. James
reminded us that if believing was all it took to walk in the
fullness of God's life, even Satan's devils would be saved.

*Thou believest that there is one God; thou doest
well: the devils also believe, and tremble. But wilt
thou know, O vain man, that faith without works
is dead?* (James 2:19–20)

Faith, the obedient response to every word of God,
is what takes us through God's step-by-step process
for becoming soldiers in life. Romans 10:17 says, *"Faith
cometh by hearing, and hearing by the word of God."* But
it is the obedient response to every word of God that
puts flesh on the bones of our Christian walk from glory
to glory and faith to faith.

*For I am not ashamed of the gospel of Christ: for
it is the power of God unto salvation to every one*

that believeth; to the Jew first, and also to the Greek. For therein is the righteousness of God revealed from faith to faith: as it is written, The just shall live by faith. (Romans 1:16–17)

BROKEN LIVES METHOD

Are you having a hard time picturing yourself as a soldier? Are you having difficulty hearing and accepting God's potential for your life?

Remember, Ezekiel 37:2 says the bones were dry and without life. God will move in lifeless situations. He is always ready to impart His Spirit to any who will confess the dryness and deadness of their lives. Just because you have a hard time picturing yourself as a life-filled fighting soldier in God's army doesn't mean it won't happen. Ezekiel's prophetic picture shows how the broken pieces of our lives come together in God's special mending once we accept and obey His sovereign Word.

So I prophesied as I was commanded: and as I prophesied, there was a noise, and behold a shaking, and the bones came together, bone to his bone. (Ezekiel 37:7)

God's mending process is not always easy. If we are to become God's powerful army, we first have to be shaken out of everything that is not of God. We need to be shaken out of our comfort zones of denominational doctrines and rulebooks; we need to be torn away from sin, witchcraft, evil doings, jealousy, and division. His Holy Spirit will do it once you respond to His Word. And when God begins to speak to you, He will mend your broken dreams. There will be a shaking as the pieces of your life come back together to form His image of you. As He brought Ezekiel's broken bones together to form a powerful army, He will gather the dead, dry pieces of your life and breathe His life-changing Spirit into them.

> *Then said he unto me, Prophesy unto the wind, prophesy, son of man, and say to the wind, Thus saith the Lord GOD; Come from the four winds, O breath, and breathe upon these slain, that they may live.* (Ezekiel 37:9)

Notice that the wind of God's Spirit in Ezekiel's vision came from the four winds, or the four corners of the earth. Ezekiel's prophetic vision encourages us to know that there isn't any area of our lives that God can't fill with His Holy Spirit. God's Word will speak truth into our spirits universally. Our broken pasts, our loneliness, our wounds, and our disappointments can all be healed—restored and made brand-new from the north, south, east, and west.

More of Him

WHEN GOD BEGINS TO SPEAK TO YOU, HE WILL MEND YOUR BROKEN DREAMS.

The Spirit of God will tell you to live. His truth will speak into your barrenness and cause your womb to open. He will tell you to be healed, encourage you when you're discouraged, speak hope when you're hopeless, and bring life out of death. The Comforter, Teacher, Helper, and Guide will come to whosoever calls upon

Him. He will make them new creatures with born-again lives.

Focus on what you hear from God instead of the negatives that float around you every day. Know that the Holy Spirit will fill and renew the dry, dead areas of your life. Report every day for new instructions as a soldier in God's army. Open yourself to His gifts. Don't forbid the gift of tongues. Be available to receive His gift of prophecy and other spiritual gifts. Be sensitive when God may be sending someone to you with an encouraging word. Look for His truth daily in the pages of Scripture. And, above all, stay in order. As you grow from faith to faith, He will use you to breathe new life into others. He will keep you fresh within the powerful, peaceful flow of His mighty rushing wind. And God will receive the glory as He completes His work through us.

Afterword

THE BENEFITS OF DIVINE CONNECTION

Afterword

THE BENEFITS OF DIVINE CONNECTION

e've done extensive coverage concerning the value of having a divine connection with God. We've learned who the Holy Spirit really is, what it means to be saved, and the different forms of baptism. We've learned that water baptism is not something to be used as a tool for salvation, but it announces that you've already received Christ as Lord and Savior. The Word of God is simple and is not to be confused by religious jargon and philosophies according to mankind's private interpretations. Remember that the devil will use any door that he possibly can to confuse your thinking concerning spiritual matters by complicating the simplicity of the God's Word. Just as He used God's word to beguile Eve in the Garden of Eden, he will do the same thing today to those who seek to know the Lord in a more intimate way.

> *But I fear, lest by any means, as the serpent beguiled Eve through his subtlety, so your minds should be corrupted from the simplicity that is in Christ.* (2 Corinthians 11:3)

191

Although we know the truth, we're often inadvertently led astray when we take time to listen to the opinions of others without having a spiritual foundation that is strong enough to endure the fake doctrines that come to shake our faith. Time and again, as I teach the Word of God, I've seen the bewilderment of faces that have been taught things that have no merit or validity in the Word of God. To be shown the truth can be quite an eye-opening experience. This is why baptisms are a part of the believer's life and are such an unforgettable experience. Whether you're being baptized in water or baptized in the Holy Spirit, both instances require you to be fully immersed and then exposed with a more in-depth and eye-opening revelation of God's spirit. We often feel that if we don't fall out in the spirit or quicken that God is not with us. You should never allow the experience of another individual to become the pattern for how you feel your spiritual walk in Christ should manifest.

To be connected in Christ is much more than an emotional experience, but it is an inexplicable miracle. In being connected to Him you do not have to conjure up emotionalism, but the evidence of a life surrendered to Him will be revealed to those who come in contact with you. The Spirit of God is so powerful that He often speaks through you without uttering a word. It is the love of God shown through you that becomes a contagious attraction to those who come in contact with you. It is also what provokes the anger of the enemy. When he sees that you're no longer moved by the outside influences that once caused you to stray away from God, he will intensify his pursuit. Because the Spirit of God is with you, however, you can remain victorious.

THE BENEFITS OF DIVINE *Connection*

We've learned throughout the preceding chapters the necessity of God's Spirit, but for clarification, let us review the pertinence of who He truly is and how to draw nigh to Him.

SALVATION

The first step to gaining a closer walk with God is in submitting your life to Him wholeheartedly. In an old familiar hymn, the songwriter asks, "What can wash away my sins?" and then responded, "Nothing but the blood of Jesus!" Although it has been erroneously taught within some doctrines that water baptism saves, nothing can wash away the sins of the world except the blood of Jesus Christ. Salvation is simply a process of confession and belief : *"If thou shalt confess with thy mouth the Lord Jesus, and shalt believe in thine heart that God hath raised him from the dead, thou shalt be saved"* (Romans 10:9).

RELATIONSHIP

Subsequent to salvation you will then begin to develop a more intimate relationship with God. As you get to know Him and cling to His Word, you will begin to notice changes in your spiritual appetite. The things that once consumed your thought processes become of less importance because the Spirit of God is keeping your mind at perfect peace. Perfect peace does not mean a life without challenges, but it implies that, regardless of the situation, the Lord will allow you to experience His peace in the midst of the storm. Your life outwardly begins to reflect the inward change that has taken place. Then you decide that you'd like to be baptized. There are two forms of baptism—baptism in water and baptism in the Holy Spirit.

BAPTISM IN WATER

The sprinkling of water or the submersion into water is not a tool for salvation. Instead, the water becomes a symbolic grave: Being baptized in water represents the burial of that body, and rising out of the water represents resurrection—dying to this world and rising to walk in the newness of life.

Baptism is an outward sign of the inward work that has taken place in the life of the believer. Understanding baptism through study takes the chilly water and turns it into a river of life, springing up from everlasting to everlasting. We need to understand, though, the difference between baptism in the Holy Spirit and being filled with the Holy Spirit: these are two separate experiences. Before our salvation, the Holy Spirit convicts us of sin and introduces us to Christ Jesus. The work of the filling of the Holy Spirit, however, begins at redemption.

BAPTISM IN THE HOLY SPIRIT

Before Jesus was baptized in water by John the Baptist, John told the people:

I indeed baptize you with water unto repentance: but he that cometh after me is mightier than I,

*whose shoes I am not worthy to bear: he shall
baptize you with the Holy Ghost, and with fire.*
(Matthew 3:11)

Although John baptized the people in water, he
wanted the people to know that a Power much greater
than him was coming onto the scene to baptize them
with power in the form of the Holy Spirit. John did not
want them to become complacent subsequent to being
baptized in water and hinder the full manifestation of
the Holy Spirit.

*Then Peter said unto them, Repent, and be bap-
tized every one of you in the name of Jesus Christ
for the remission of sins, and ye shall receive the
gift of the Holy Ghost.* (Acts 2:38)

Receiving the baptism of the Holy Spirit is your
supernatural immersion in the Spirit of God. As long
as you are saved, you can get to heaven without being
water baptized, but at the same time, you will have
robbed yourself of experiencing God's miraculous power
and limited the full manifestation of your spiritual experience. Although it is the Holy Spirit who convicts you
and allows you to receive salvation, He does not force
Himself into your life after you are saved. Just as being
baptized in water is a choice and a decision you make,
so it is with receiving the baptism of the Holy Spirit.

*In the last day, that great day of the feast, Jesus
stood and cried, saying, If any man thirst, let him
come unto me, and drink. He that believeth on
me, as the scripture hath said, out of his belly
shall flow rivers of living water.* (John 7:37–38)

195

The Holy Spirit is not a dogmatic dictator, but He is a Comforter. During difficult times when you feel that you can't go on, the Holy Spirit comes to remind you, "You can make it." If you believe on Him, He will quench your thirst and allow the rivers of living water to flow from your belly, filling your appetite with His glory and power. The Holy Spirit gives you the power to engage in spiritual warfare in a capacity that is unknown to those who are without Him. Your boldness forces you to confront the demons of your past, cast down every stronghold, and have victory over many of the things that have kept you on the run.

Another attribute to those who have the Holy Spirit is the love of Christ. His godly love is exhibited in action and not by words. They possess a discipline to submit to leadership that keeps them in God's divine will, which is why the blessings of God often overtake them. They're not defeated by conflict, but see it as another opportunity for God to be glorified. This is because, when you possess the Holy Spirit, your foresight is sharpened. You can spot oncoming attacks and realize that you must defeat them, not by carnal weapons, but by the mighty weapons of God and with the power that He has endowed to you from on high. The same weapon that Jesus used to defeat the devil, is what we must use today—the Word of God. *"But he answered and said, It is written, Man shall not live by bread alone, but by every word that proceedeth out of the mouth of God"* (Matthew 4:4).

You have to know the Word of God. The devil knows Scripture and he also knows how to twist it in order to use it against you. When you've spent time with God, however, you learn how to combat the strategies of the devil and overcome every trap that he has set for your demise.

The Holy Spirit is a conduit into the supernatural, and besides being a Comforter, He serves many purposes:

1. Witnessing: the Holy Spirit gives us the power to be His witnesses, spreading the gospel of Jesus Christ. *"But ye shall receive power, after that the Holy Ghost is come upon you: and ye shall be witnesses unto me"* (Acts 1:8). This Scripture is powerful because it shows the power of God's Spirit, which gives us the ability to be a witness unto Jesus Christ and not to our individual doctrines and opinions.

2. Our Supernatural Leader: He serves as a guide into the supernatural, allowing us to experience revelation that would otherwise remain hidden from our carnal mind-sets and way of thinking. *"Howbeit when he, the Spirit of truth, is come, he will guide you into all truth... and he will show you things to come"* (John 16:13). Without God's supernatural insight we'd continue to stumble upon the enemy's battlefield and become ambushed by his brutal attacks.

3. In Our Prayer Life: Have you ever bowed to pray for a need, but didn't quite know how to articulate it to God? This is where the Holy Spirit comes in: *"Likewise the Spirit also helpeth our infirmities: for we know not what we should pray for as we ought: but the Spirit itself maketh intercession for us with groanings which cannot be uttered"* (Romans 8:26). What better Person to intercede on our behalf than the One who also knows how to answer our prayers.

4. Our Teacher: Just as we need teachers in the natural, we also need the spiritual teachings of Jesus Christ in order to illuminate our thinking and keep us in remembrance of God's Word: *"But the Comforter, which is the Holy Ghost, whom the Father will send in my name, he shall teach you all things, and bring all things to your remembrance, whatsoever I have said unto you"* (John 14:26).

5. Uniting Us as One: God's total purpose is unity in Christ Jesus. Regardless of our denominations, ethnicity, race, sex, or creed, there remains only one God. It is the Holy Spirit that introduces us to Him and allows us to become partakers of His divine will. *"For by one Spirit are we all baptized into one body, whether we be Jews or Gentiles, whether we be bond or free; and have been all made to drink into one Spirit"* (1 Corinthians 12:13).

Whether you're being baptized in water or in the Spirit, both are spiritual encounters with His power that you should never rob yourself of experiencing. Baptism allows you to let go of ungodly spirits, freeing you to hear the voice of God with clarity and understanding. It is your confession of Christ that allows these sins to remain buried, never to be resurrected again. Whenever you feel these issues or ungodly spirits trying to creep back into your life, you need simply to speak the Word! Confess that your baptism was more than a chilly experience, that now you're walking in newness of life.

THE BENEFITS OF DIVINE *Connection*

When you receive baptism into your life, you are going to begin receiving divine revelation. And this divine revelation will reveal to you truths that God could not share with you beforehand. Baptism brings you into the body of Christ, connecting you with other believers. It is through baptism that God knits His children together into a unified body.

Before I really understood baptism, I was baptized in water four or five times. Once I got it right, though, I realized that there were some things God wanted to tell me and show me that He couldn't reveal to me beforehand. Baptism is not a ritual but is indeed a spiritual experience with God. Although you may still have issues that you need to deal with after baptism, you will soon see the doorway of revelation that God has been trying to show you. Baptism will unlock every prison door in your life. Baptism connects you with God. Don't underestimate its many benefits.

In realizing the many benefits that are attached to a life submitted to the voice and will of God, you will begin to see the manifestation of His power as never before. Your struggle to let go of the things that have been holding you back will become easier to relinquish into the capable hands of God. As you decrease, you will experience the power of His might while He reveals the strengths that you never knew even existed.

About the Author

GEORGE BLOOMER

ishop George G. Bloomer is a native of Brooklyn, New York. After serving as an evangelist for fourteen years, Dr. Bloomer began pastoring in 1996. He is the founder and senior pastor of Bethel Family Worship Center in Durham, North Carolina, but continues to travel extensively, sharing with others his testimony of how the Lord delivered him from a life of poverty, drug abuse, sexual abuse, and mental anguish. "God had a plan for my life," Bloomer now says, "and even during my span of lawlessness, the angels of the Lord were protecting me because the call of God was upon my life."

Bloomer holds the degree of Doctor of Religious Arts in Christian Psychology and conducts many seminars dealing with relationships, finances, and stress management. He is founder of Young Witnesses for Christ, a youth evangelistic outreach ministry with several chapters on college campuses throughout the United States, and bishop of C.L.U.R.T (Come Let Us Reason Together) International Assemblies, comprised of over 80 churches nationwide and abroad. His message is one of deliverance and of a hope that far exceeds the desperation and oppression of many silent sufferers.